JOOMLA! 1.5 & Virtuemart:

The Power is at your Fingertips

CorporationGURU Books

Other great books from CorporationGURU and Michelle M. Griffin, PhD (abd)

The Joomla books are part of the "Elephants Can't Change" series in order to assist corporations and business to become agile instead of participating in the "invent it here syndrome"

Business Books

Elephant's Can't Change but Leopards Can!!! (2008)
Strategic Organization Development Roadmap (2008)
Employ!!! Performance (2008)

Computer/Web Design Books

Joomla! 1.5 & Virtuemart: The Power is at your Fingertips
Joomla! 1.5 & Virtuemart for Sports Clubs (2008)
Joomla! 1.5 & Virtuemart for Not for Profits (2008)
Joomla! 1.5 & Virtuemart for Catalog (2008)
Joomla! 1.5 & Virtuemart for Schools (2008)
Joomla! 1.5 & Virtuemart for Restaurants (2008)
Joomla! 1.5 & Virtuemart for Corporations (2008)
Joomla!1.5 & Virtuemart for Health Care (2008)

Fiction Books

Mafia: Dead Bosses are Back for Revenge! (2008)

Available on Amazon

Joomla 1.5 & Virtuemart:

The Power is in your Fingertips!

Michelle M. Griffin, PhD (abd)

Corporation Guru Inc.
www.corporationguru.com
Delaware * Chicago * Orlando

BookSurge Publishing
North Charleston, South Carolina

Library of Congress Cataloging Control Number -2008906716
Griffin PhD, Michelle
Joomla! 1.5 & Virtuemart: The Power is at your Fingertips by Michelle M. Griffin, PhD
Includes bibliographical references.
p. cm.
ISBN 1-4392-0404-7
1. Griffin PhD, Michelle 1963- .
2. Management – United States.
3. Computers
4. Internet
5: Web Design
I. Title

CorporationGuru books are available at special quantity discounts to use as premiums and sales promotions or for use in corporate training programs. For more information, please visit the www.corporationguru.com.

The author and publisher specifically disclaim any liability that is incurred from the application of the contents of this book.

The editor for this book was Christine L. Banerjee
It was set by CorporationGRAPHIC, www.corporationgraphic.com.

ISBN:1-4392-0404-7
Library of Congress Control Number: 2008906716
Visit www.booksurge.com to order additional copies.
Published by BookSurge Publishing North Charleston, South Carolina
co-Published by CorporationGuru, Chicago, Illinois.
First Edition, July 2008

Dedication

To all the Open Source Developers who are changing and shaping the future of this world. With this I am donating 5% of profits from this book, each month to an Open Source Not for Profit organization.

If you find you use Joomla or Virtuemart or any other Open Source component. Please donate to these organizations, for the continued development of the Open Source platform.

TABLE OF CONTENTS

FIGURES

Contents

Introduction

This book is written for the person or corporation, who has little experience with website design. Too many corporations and businesses are re-inventing the wheel. Right in front of you is the most awesome tool available to develop a presence on the internet. It is called Open Source. You don't have to continue to hire people to maintain and develop your website, I don't care how complicated it is. Open Source just made it easier to modify and change your website.

What is a content management system?

A content management system is a package of Internet software applications, which allow you to take full control over your website without any knowledge of html, UNIX or PHP. Whether you are a large corporation, a not for profit, entrepreneur or a sport team, open source content management puts the power at your finger tips to be as simple or complex as you can imagine.

The content management system is database driven, using an SQL database you can now have people register online, send newsletters to your customer database and email your customers, all through your website. No more separate databases maintaining customer records. If you are a small company and have not ventured into the large ERP software packages like SAP or Oracle, you can conduct all your business through a content management system. We will describe a package called Virtuemart an ecommerce tool to track inventory and sales.

The most fantastic thing about content management systems you can use forms on your website, you can add, edit, delete and manage data and content; build a community, have a picture gallery, latest news, post careers, create and manage the design and structure of your site and its navigation system; include images the abilities of a content management system are endless and it is right there at your finger tips.

Joomla and other products we describe in this book are not for profit companies. They need your support. If you are a business reading this book and you saved yourself a $60,000 dollar employee, why not donate some of that money back so the Open Source Revolution can continue. When you are through with this book, you will have a fantastic website which is as simple or complicated as you want.

In the book "Elephants Can't Change but Leopards Can!!!" available on Amazon. I made fun of corporations and how in order to survive in the future they have to be agile and stop the "Invent it here syndrome". This is the first book in the series to teach corporations to be agile. All corporations from the solo proprietorship to the largest Elephant Corporation needs to grab on to Open Source, the future is not in large IT departments in these Virtual corporations, where the brightest are creating a revolution that most people have missed so far.

With this book, you will have a working website up within less than an hour with full ecommerce functionality if you desire. This book is a step by step process to achieve a beautiful looking website without spending a lot of money.

So how much does it cost to build a website, basically only whatever you pay your webhoster per month and the person you have maintaining your website. Webhosting ranges from $5.95 -$40 a month for shared hosting to full dedicated servers running $500 a month for large corporations.

This book is put out by a webhoster located at www.spiderweby. com. We are a full service webhoster. The reason we are writing this book, is to help people join the internet without causing stress.

There is a small learning curve, but nothing overwhelming, in fact you will find exhilaration and satisfaction in doing something the world can see.

Again, This is the wonderful thing about open source, it is free. But, the developers of Joomla and the other open source software would love for you to give a donation to their organizations. Because without their hard work, you would be paying $1000's of dollars to build the same functionality they have enabled you to have within less than an hour. Therefore please donate to all the great open source organizations, some we will document in this book.

You are thinking, Cool, I always wanted a website. But, then stress kicks in and you begin to wonder:
- What will the website be about?
- What will my name be?
- Where do I start?
- Am I selling something or just having people call me?
- How do I make it look nice?
- How do I get visitors to hit my site?

Don't fret, we will walk you through the process from beginning to end and it will be fun while you are doing it. We are also assuming you have used the internet before and you are familiar with going to Google or Yahoo and searching for an item.

So let's get started, we are going to start with the basics, so if you are a little more advance then skip to the chapter you have not completed.

Website (Domain) Name

The first thing you need to do is buy a domain name. Now there are a ton of domain names out there. But you may not be able to buy the first name you want because it may already be taken. Be creative and come up with a number of different names. I actually go out to www.Dotster.com and type in domain names until I find one I like.

There are a few keys to creating a domain name:
• Keep it memorable – your customers need something they can spell and remember.

• Keep it short as possible, the longer it is the easier to misspell as they are trying to find your site. When a website is spelled wrong it either drops out to a Ask.com – which is irritating, because you can't go back. Ask locks you in the site or it drops you out to a company which slams you with viruses because you typed something close to the name of a famous company. Either way try to make it easy on your customers to find you.

• Be descriptive, many times I will use parts of words to make up the site name. For instance, the name of the holding corporation for Spiderweby is Center for Economies of Change Corporation. I found that CEO.com was taken, CEOC. com was taken therefore I purchased www.centereoc.com, economiesochange.com and ceochange.com. I purchased all three, because I wanted flexibility in what name I was going to use, since I was undecided in the beginning. Now I just use www. centereoc.com with economiesofchange.com and ceochange.com as redirects to www.centereoc.com.

Do you see how I took the name and developed different

variations which are still descriptive of the name?

When you do a test search for your domain name, you will see all kind of extensions. These different extensions exist in order to make the internet more organized. These domain extensions are known as top level domain name (TLDN). Pages from a website then are represented after the domain name; for instance, www.centereoc.com/index or www.centeroc.com/customer.   Below are the current domain extensions, just to name a few:
- .com – are commercial enterprises from small businesses to large corporations
- .edu – are educational institutions
- .gov – are government organizations
- .mil – are military organizations
- .net – are network and webhosting organizations
- .org – are non profit organizations
- .info – are for informational sites
- .mobi – are mobile device websites
- .biz – are for commercial organizations also but the .com is still the most common selection for commercial use.
- .us – are United States websites
- .tv – are news stations and video sites
- .name- are intended for use for people's real names
- .jobs – this is restricted to employment related sites.
- .travel – classifies travel related sites.

There are also country domain names which you will run across the more you use the internet. A few common country domain name extensions, found regularly on the internet:
- .ca – Canda
- .cn – China
- .de – Germany
- .dk – Denmark
- .es – Spain

- .fi – Finland
- .fr – France
- .gb or .uk – United Kingdom
- .hk – Hong Kong
- .it – Italy
- .in – India
- .jp – Japan
- .mx – Mexico
- .ru – Russia
- .se – Sweden

Once you settle on a name and you find it available you have to register the name. All domain names are registered through ICANN (Internet Corporation for Assigned Names and Numbers). But you can't purchase directly from ICANN, you have to go through a registrar. There are hundreds of registrars. If you would like to look one up, you can go to www.internic.net which is the register for all domain resellers. Again, I just use Dotster, since I have been using them for years and have had zero issues with them.

To register your domain, you need to buy it. This requires you to use your credit card and sign up online or over the phone. It is a pretty straight forward process. Just watch that you are paying for the time frame you want the domain name, meaning 1 year, 2 years or 3 years. Some companies force you to the 3 year but you need to change it to the length you want. Just realize, if you sign up for only a year, next year you have to renew the domain name. If you forget, because you don't use the email address any longer you signed up with, you will lose your name. It is awful to lose a name which you have built a relationship on it.

Also remember nothing is truly free.   There are a lot of

companies which will give you a free domain name with a one year webhosting. Once you leave this webhoster they have locked your name and you either have to stay with them to keep it or change your domain name all together. It is better to pay regular price for your domain and not be locked in. A normal domain name costs $10 to $20 dollars with no restrictions.

Once you lost your domain name, the bulk domain buyers buy it up and you then sometimes have to pay hundreds of dollars to get it back. This is very important to remember, your domain name is critical don't allow yourself to lose it by not paying attention to the expiration.

Also, many domain registrars will try to add additional services like web hosting or who is privacy to your domain name registration. You can delete these; you do not have to buy all the services. Just ensure it shows the domain name and anything else you want to purchase.

Once you have purchase your domain, your registrar should send you an email with the registration and how to log in and change the Nameservers. The nameservers are critical these are what tells the internet where your website can be found. The nameserver is usually tied to your webhosters IP address unless you contracted for your own IP address.

You receive your nameserver names from your webhoster. There are typically two nameservers they are for instance: ns1. centereoc.net and ns2.centereoc.net.

At the back of this book, I have included a coupon for 3 months free webhosting, in order for you to learn how to build your website and then decide your future. I have tried to remove the stress of learning something new, without having to navigate through all the webhosters, trying to figure out which one is best.

If you decide to use the 3 month coupon the nameservers are:
ns1.centereoc.net
ns2.centereoc.net.

Therefore go to the next chapter to begin to see how to sign up for a webhoster.

Special note: Now, in order to rank better in SEO (Search Engine Optimization) it is better to have your own IP address tied to your name servers. This way you are seen as a separate entity away from your webhoster. The dedicated IP address is extra money, but it is worth it. The IP address can run from $5 to $50 dollars a year depending on who are hosting with. Do this down the road, don't do it right this minute. With the new features in Joomla 1.5 many sites do not need dedicated IP address as they did in the past.

Finding a Webhoster

People, who are looking for webhosting for the first time, will find it overwhelming. So let's start from the beginning.

Web Hosting Types

The first question to think about is what type of site you are going to be maintaining. Most first timers start with a shared webhoster service. This runs around $6.95 a month to $20.00 a month based on what you are looking for. Given the competition between hosting companies you can find a good webhoster at $6.95 a month. Spiderweby (www.spiderweby.com) tries to stay cost competitive with other webhosters. Remember we offer a coupon for 3 month of free webhosting.

The most basic web hosting is called Shared Web hosting: What this means is a company has a server (web host) and they rent you space on their server. On one web server there could be 1000's of sites; all sharing the same resources like RAM, bandwidth and operating systems. Don't be scared, servers can host all these websites with no problems and there are administrators in the background ensuring that no one website steals too much space from the other.

Your webhoster needs to have the following in order for you to have control of your website:

• It must have CPANEL; this is your command center for your website. By having cpanel you are able to setup email accounts, redirect domains, park domains and maintain your sql servers as well as access the root (system files) area of your website. Many webhosters include it free and some charge for the use of it. Try to find one which includes it. Figure 1, shows what a CPANEL looks like.

Figure 1: Cpanel Display

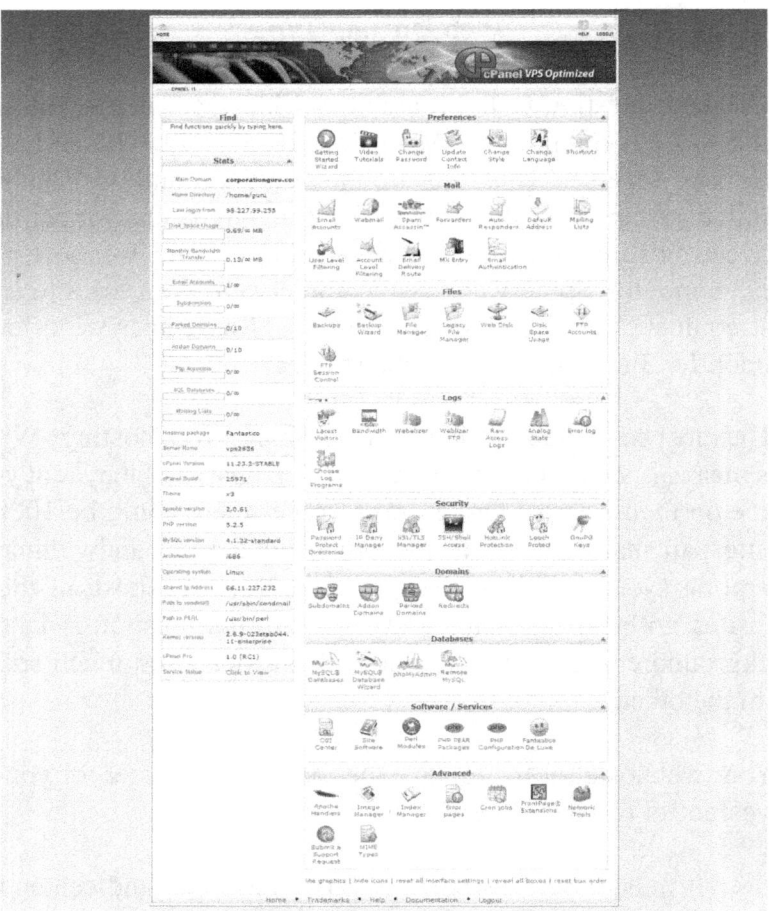

• Storage: You also need a webhoster who gives you at minimum 1,500 gig storage but preferably unlimited storage.

•   Data Transfer Rate: Industry standard is 15,000 gigs data transfer per month (this should serve just about anyone's needs who do not require their own virtual private server).

•   Database: In order to install Joomla, you need SQL database ability. Preferably they give you unlimited databases. Even though most people only use a few.

•   Emails: 50 to unlimited emails addresses are pretty standard with most services.

•   FANTASTICO, this is critical. You do not want to maintain and install Joomla the manual way. FANTASTICO keeps up to date on the latest versions of Joomla. The process of installation is extremely easy, with FANTASTICO. Some webhosters give it free and some charge for it.

•   You need to be able to FTP files to your servers. This allows you to change images and change logos.

Those are the most critical things you need with a webhoster in order to easily build your site. One last thing, you need which is nice to have, is root access to your file manager. If you go back to Figure 1: cpanel, you notice there is a file manager. You need to be able to make the configuration file writable in order to update it this is critical to SEO (Search Engine Optimization), which we will discuss in another chapter.

Special note: Check how long it takes once you subscribe to the webhosting service to setup your account. It can take from 1 hour to 10 days, depending on the webhoster. If you are like me, patience is not a virtue and I want it done fast.

For beginners, they fall into the trap of the cheapest, but then get nickel and dimed to death. You want a Webhoster with a low per month cost, which includes cpanel, good disk space, sql databases, with adequate bandwidth and fantastico.

Your main concern is availability and how quickly can the technical team recover you from an error. Be forewarned, though many hosting companies will charge through the nose for rebuilding your site for you. If you follow the guidelines throughout the book, you will be fine. It is when you learn a little and you begin experimenting that your site crashes or takes a long time to load.

There are other types of hosting, which we will explain high level, you will need to be a more advanced user to utilized these options. Once you venture down these paths, I have found very few webhosters willing to help you through the learning curve. Therefore I recommend you stay with shared services, until you get your feet wet.

The other services are a VPS (Virtual Private Server) or a Dedicated Server. The VPS runs roughly ($40 dollars a month to $100 a month).

A VPS is a server (computer) which is partitioned into multiple servers. Each segment appearance and capabilities simulate that of a stand alone server. Each VPS is considered independent and can be rebooted. The nice thing about VPS is that you have root access to control your files. But, there is a lot more responsibilities to maintaining a VPS. With a VPS everything is extra Cpanel and Plesk (server administration). There is a much longer learning curve. My recommendation if you are going to use VPS then get it with CPANEL, because it is much easier to maintain individual sites with it. Then use the Plesk for server maintenance and backups. If you are a demanding web user, many webhosters many force you to a VPS, since you take up to much server space, server bandwidth or server resources. Be forewarned running a VPS is very demanding.

Another option is the DEDICATED SERVER, this is where you lease an entire server not shared with anyone. The most powerful web hosting service is this method, which costs roughly $75-$500 a month. This option is similar to being your own Information Technology department, you find in corporations. This requires someone who understands Apache Servers, PHP, SQL and how to maintain a server.

My last recommendation, is whatever webhoster you choose, sign up for a month of service, if you like them then continue to pay by the month or by the year. If you don't then switch, now that is a pain if you spent a lot of time building your website, but in the end it is better to find a webhoster which fits your needs. I would actually by the .com, .net and .org versions of the domain names. Then if one webhoster turned out to be no good, I would sign up with another webhoster, rebuild the site with the .net domain name then when done, redirect and park the .com website to the .net. This way the site was never down until I found the right fit.

I have used a lot of web services, and could not find one that gave me everything I need. Therefore this is how Spiderweby started, in order to ensure our servers had the requirements we were looking for. My groups are very demanding, and this is also why when customers subscribe with us, we give many of the same functionality we require to the customers.

JOOMLA! Hosting Requirements

This book is written for Joomla! 1.5. The following are the settings required of your webhoster in order for Joomla to work:

- PHP 4.2.x or above
- MySQL 3.23.x or above
- Apache 1.3.x or above
- XML Must be enabled through your PHP installation
- Zlib must be enabled through your PHP installation
- You need root access to modify your .htaccess file, your folders when adding custom files and configuration file.
- Must be able to execute PHP scripts.
- Mod_Rewrite module within PHP

Subscribing to a Hosting Service

This is relatively straight forward. Typically you fill out an online form or have to call a number. You will need to give a credit card to pay either by the month or the year. This credit card stays on file with the webhoster for them to bill monthly or yearly they will send you a notice for you to go online and repay.

Some hosting companies offer free domain names with one year of service. Other companies have you pay for your domain names. Domain names range in price from Free to $15.00 with renewal every year. Even though it says free, you need to check the portability of the name if you leave that webhoster. You also need to be able to ensure you can change the nameserver if you leave the webhoster also. Some domain name providers make it very difficult to leave or change if you are hosting with them. I myself use Dotster. They are reliable and you have full access to modify your domain name servers. I prefer to keep my webhosting and domains separate.

Once you subscribe to a service, it usually takes anywhere from 1 hour to 7 days for your webhosting company to set up your server.

Note once you sign up with a webhoster, you need the name server address then you have to go back to your Domain registrar log into your account and change the name server.

This is what it looks like on Dotster, since this is where I host my domains. Note the section which states name servers, you have to click the link Update Name Servers. Then enter your nameservers, click add and then enter the second name server press add then enter your email address. Name servers always begin with ns1.webhosteruniquename.net or com and ns1. webhosteruniquename.net or com. For example, the nameservers for Spiderweby are ns1.centereoc.net and ns2.centereoc.net

Figure 2: Name Servers

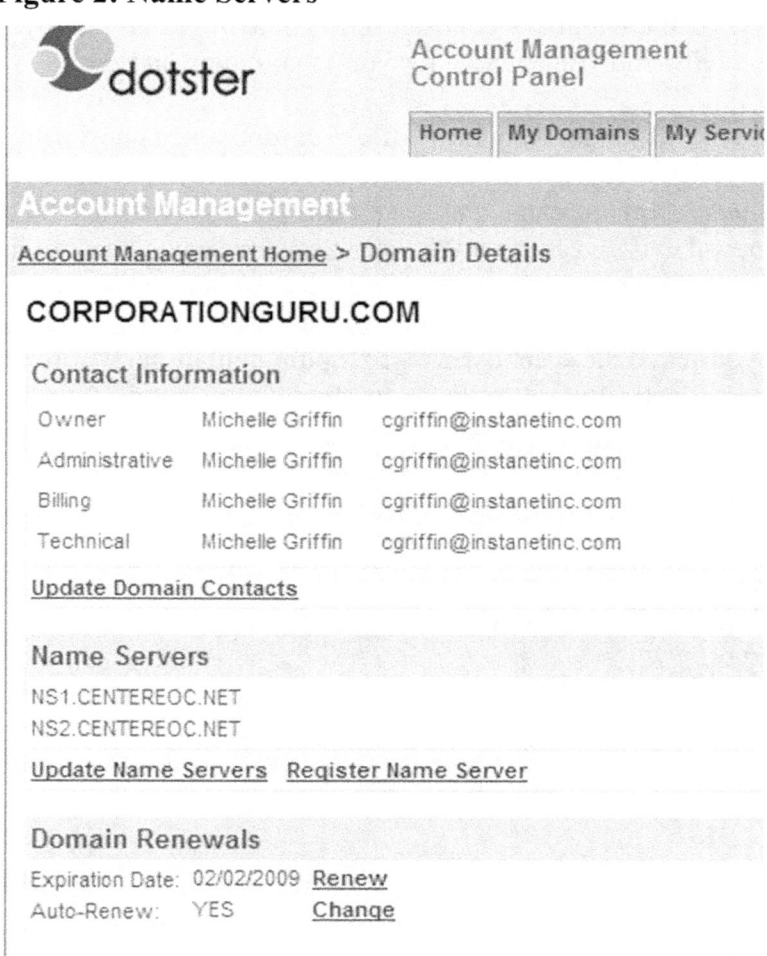

Using the Cpanel

While you are waiting on the nameserver to resolve, this takes anywhere from 24 hours to 2 days; you can begin building your website. The first time you enter the Cpanel the "Getting Started wizard" appears. Play it the first time, it gives a general overview of the Cpanel.

Next look down the side of the Cpanel there is a listing of your Disk Space Usage, Monthly Bandwidth, Number of E-mail accounts, SQL databases, Email addresses, etc…

Figure 3: Cpanel

The first to do is create an email address. Find the Mail section of your cpanel. We need to create a few email address based on your needs. I create one with my name at my domain. The others are usually a customer service account and sales account.

But you have to watch using a generic customer service or sales because it will be considered junk email in some email systems. Therefore I always come up with something that looks like a name. Instead of using customerservice@centereoc.com, I will use customer.service@centereoc.com. But really this is a personal preference how you want to label your e-mail.

Click on the email account button. Enter your email address and password. Click Create. Once the email is created it will ask you, "Do you wish to configure the account to work with an outlook client". Click YES.

Figure 4: Add Email Account

Add a New Email Account

Please Enter the User and the Password you wish to use:

Email:	@ corporationguru.com ▾
Password:	Generate Password
Password Strength:	
	Very Weak (0/100)
Password (Again):	
Mailbox quota (optional):	250 MB
	Create

Current Accounts

Search   Go

ACCOUNT	ACCESS WEBMAIL	USAGE	QUOTA	FUNCTIONS
michelle.griffin@corporationguru.com		None	250 MB	Delete Change Quota Change Password Security Policy Configure Mail Client

You can either configure Outlook to receive your email or you can read your email on line. This section is for business with out an IT department. If you have an IT department then skip over this section, contact your IT group to set up the email.

Figure 5: Outlook Configuration after you click Yes

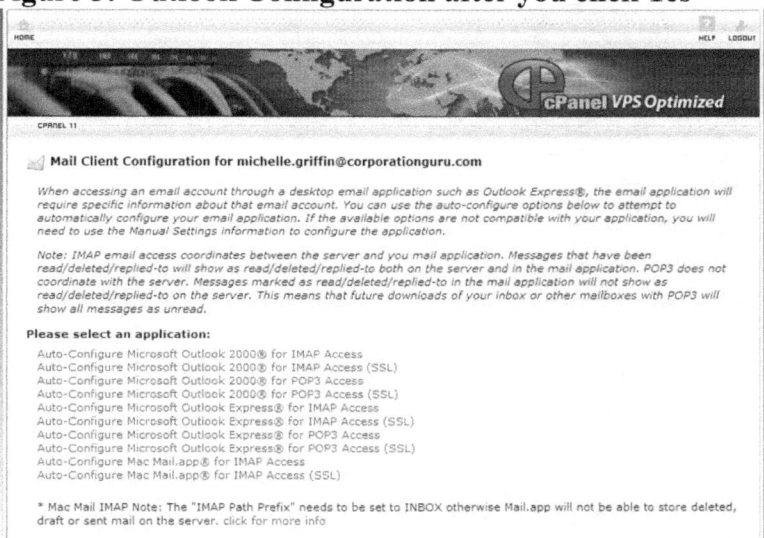

We will show you first how to configure Outlook.
Open Outlook and Select Tools/Email Accounts.
Select Add new Account and click next.

The next screen, select Pop3 and click next. A screen similar
to figure 7 will pop up.

Enter your Name
Email Address
Username created in Figure 4
Password
Incoming Pop3 - this information is found in Figure 5
Outgoing SMTP - this information is found in Figure 5

Figure 6: Add Email Account

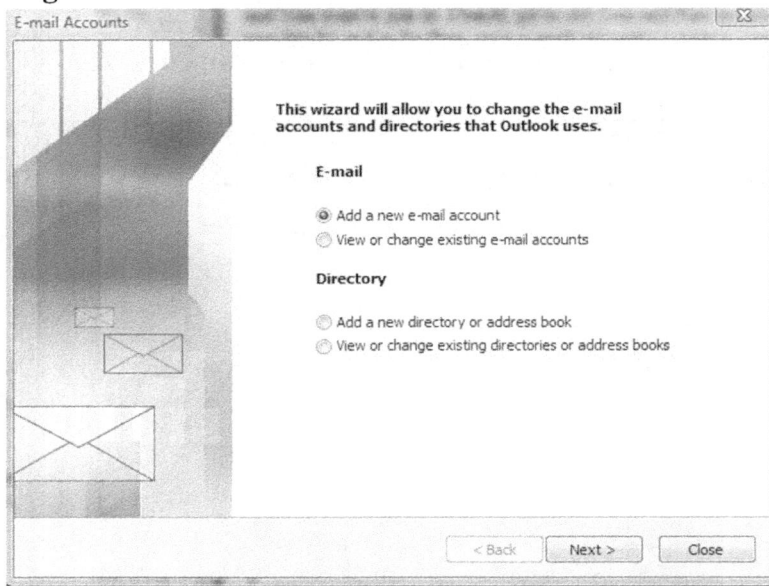

Figure 7: Enter Email

Click Test Account Settings, if everything is correct the Status will show completed.

Figure 8: Email completion

If an error comes back then something was missed spelled, go back and review the previous screen. If you find everything is spelled correctly then go back to the Cpanel and reconfigure for Outlook, described in the beginning of this section. If the Pop3 (incoming mail) shows completed, this means you are receiving your email.

If the SMTP (outgoing mail) fails, this is your local internet provider requires a username and password. Go to the next step below to enter your username and password. If you don't know it, then contact your internet provider for this information. Once it all shows completed press the close button.

Now, press the "More Settings" button. You need to give your email account a name.

Figure 9: Email Naming

Now, some of you may be using a telephone company as your internet provider. Some of these require Outgoing Server authentication (SMTP). Which is the 2nd tab, you may need to enter your username and password here. If the outgoing server fails when testing, contact your Internet provider to ask them how to setup the SMTP in Outlook.

Figure 10: Outgoing Server (SMTP)

When done click ok, you are now back to the add email screen, click next and click finished your email account is setup.

Installing Joomla!

Now, go back to your Cpanel, hopefully you left it open. If not log back in. Scroll down the screen until you find Fantastico, it is located under the Software/Services section. Open another internet screen and type in your website address. Your screen should look like this.

Figure 11: Website blank

Now the fun part! Go back to your Cpanel, and if you have not click the Fantastico button do it now.

Now don't get carried away, you can't install everything on this page. Your are trying to build a professional website, overtime you will learn what the other features are.

I will explain briefly. Your screen should look like this.

Figure 12: Fantastico Screen Shot

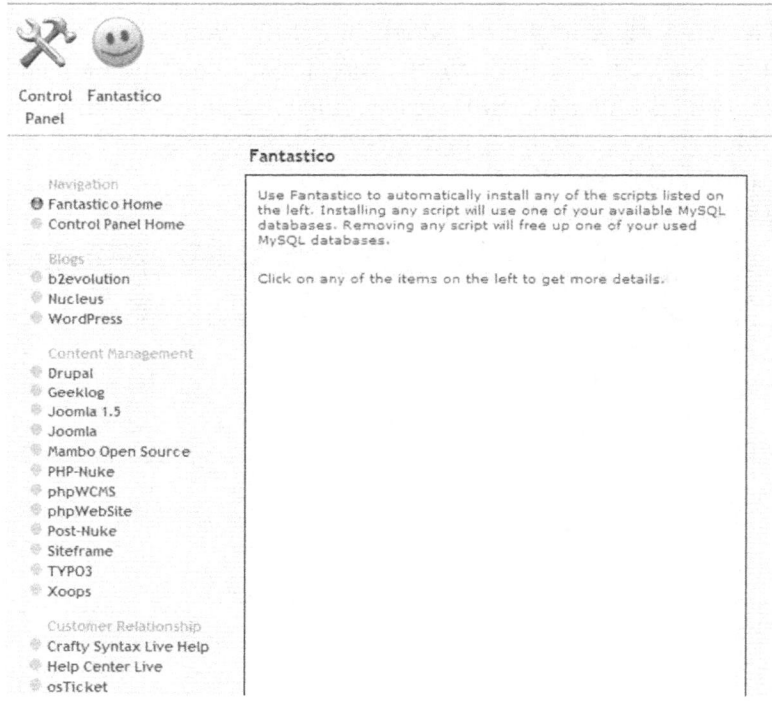

Fantastico is cool, since it installs PHP scripts for you. Now some of this stuff works together others do not. Please don't get carried away installing scripts. The section we are focused on is the Content Management.

You see Drupal, Mambo, Joomla 1.5 and others. These are all what is called content management software. It is all Open Source; some are easier to use then others. Drupal and Joomla are the industry leaders at the moment in Open Source. Drupal requires a little more IT knowledge then Joomla. Drupal and Joomla can be compared to the Apple and Microsoft companies of the world.

This book is focused on Joomla! 1.5 therefore this is what we are going to install.

Now, here it comes press the button Joomla! 1.5. The following screen appears.

Figure 13: Begin Joomla Installation

Click New Installation, the following screen appears:

Enter in your administration username and password. This is username and password you will use to enter the Joomla dashboard. Enter something you will remember.

Make sure your email address you created is in the admin email. Verify the site name. Press Install Joomla! 1.5

The following screen appears, now it will create your SQL database and install Joomla.

Figure 14: Install Joomla

Click Finish Installation.

Figure 15: Joomla Install Finish

Once the installation finishes the following screen appears:

Figure 16: Joomla Administration Information

This is information is very important, write it down or print it out and do not lose. Your access to the Joomla Dashboard is www.yourdomainname.com/administrator.

Your username and password is shown.

When finished reviewing click back to Joomla! 1.5 overview. Hurray you have done it, you created your first website, all within less than 30 minutes if you were fast.

Go back to the other internet screen and retype your domain name. Your screen has gone from being just a folder to having an actual website on it. It should look like this.

Figure 17: Your Website

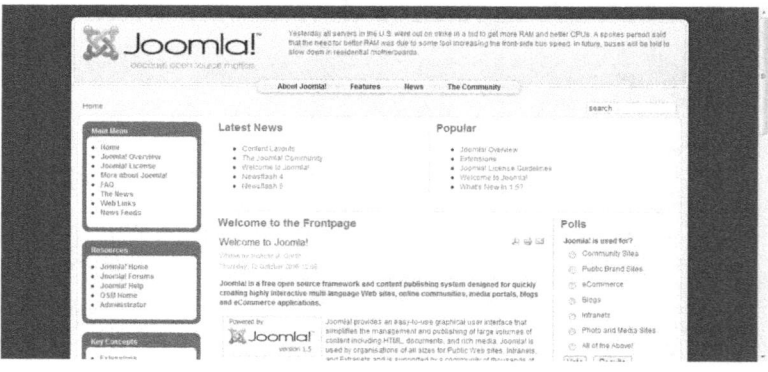

We are done with the Cpanel for now; you can close out of it. Congratulations for getting this far. Do you see how easy that was? You have conquered the first challenge, now for the fun!

Joomla Administration

Let's open a new internet session. You are going to want two internet screens open, one will be your website and the other will be the Joomla dashboard (administrator).

Go to the Joomla administrator log in screen. Enter your Username and password press login.

Note: The Joomla administrator has an automatic log out after 15 minutes. Security feature, for all your corporations, which require automatic logout.

Figure 18: Joomla administrator screen

You are now entering the Joomla dashboard. Do you see the blurbage on the right hand side, read it carefully! I will show you how to remove it, but don't remove it until you are comfortable with what it says. Security is a huge issue. Therefore when we open files and make them writable, you must remember to make them unwritable right afterwards.

Figure 19: Joomla Dashboard

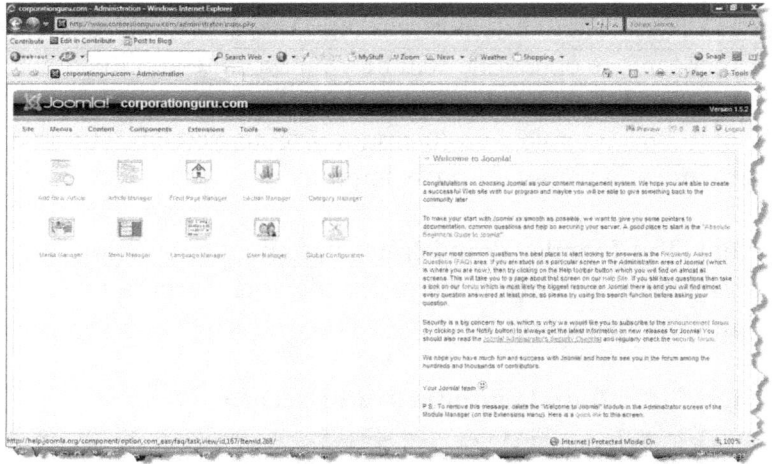

Definitely sign up for the security alerts from Joomla. This is your site, long after you finish with this book, you have to follow Joomla on developments and security warnings. Joining and participating in the forums are also good for you to go from a beginner to an advance user.

From this point forward, I will show you how to do things, in Joomla.

Try it or don't try it from this point forward it is your decision. Do you see the little green arrow next to the Welcome to Joomla, scroll down to Logged in users and click the little green arrow next to it.

It closes the other window and opens Logged in users. Below that are popular and recent added articles. Click each of the green arrows to see what information they provide.

Figure 20: Joomla Screen Right Toolbar

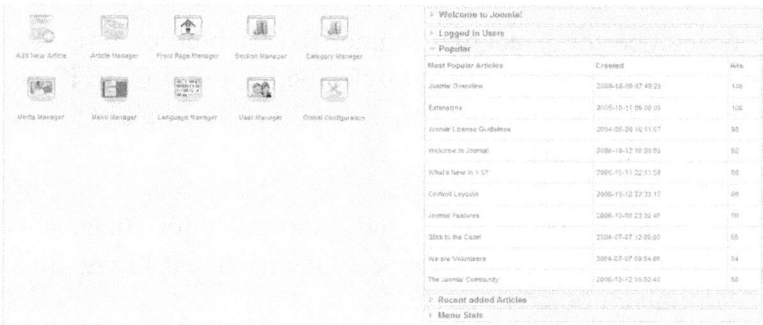

The first thing we are going to show you is how to customize your administration area. After you have read the Welcome to Joomla, I like to turn it off.

To turn it off we go to the top toolbar and highlight Extensions/ Module Manager.

Figure 21: Module Manager

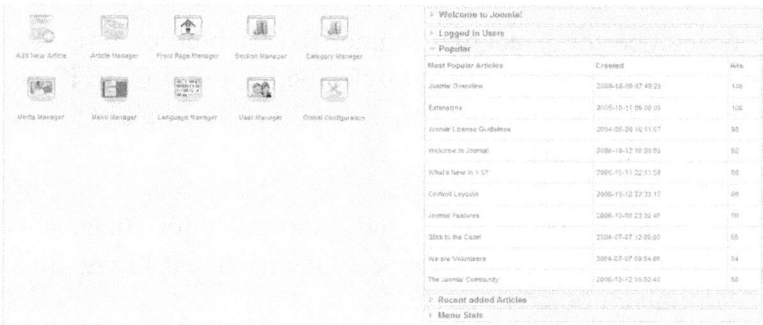

The menu manager pops up.

Do you see the checkmark under the enabled column, check marks mean enabled and red circles with an x through it means disabled. If you look just below the Module Manager name it says site or administrator.

Site means the website and Administrator means your dashboard. We are going to modify the dashboard first, click on the Administrator link.

Figure 22: Administrator Module Manager

Do you see the first line shows a module named, "Welcome to Joomla" and it shows Enabled with a check mark; we are going to disable this module.

In front of the "Welcome to Joomla" put a check in the box. On the same line as the words, Module Manager on the right there are icons. Press the disable icon. Your screen now looks

like this. Now go Site on the top toolbar and click Control panel.
Look on the right and the Welcome to Joomla is gone. Now, we
have not deleted anything, all we did is disable it and it can be
re-enabled at anytime.

So Joomla is this simple, it is just turning on and off modules
and moving things around to create a unique look.

Figure 23: Administrator disable

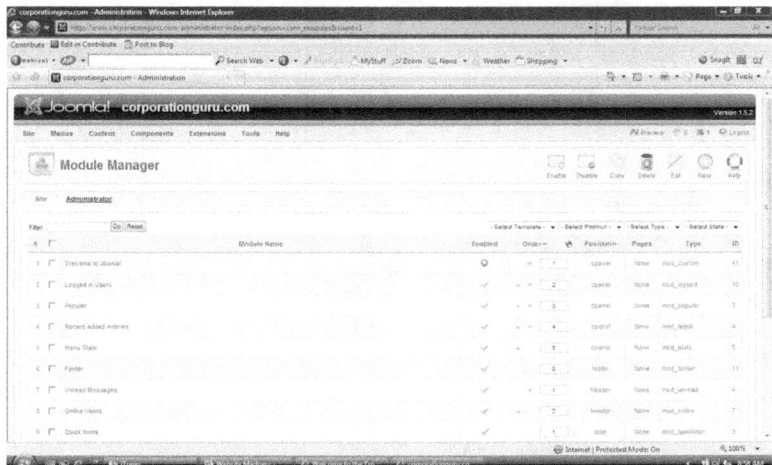

Now that we did a simple administrator change, let's change a
module on our website.

Go back to the Module manager, do you remember how?
Extensions/Module Manager

Module Manager

Module Manager turns parts of your website on and off. At least one module is required in Joomla. This is very flexible so we will start with the basics and become more advanced toward the end of the book.

You should be at the module manager screen:

Figure 24: Module Manager

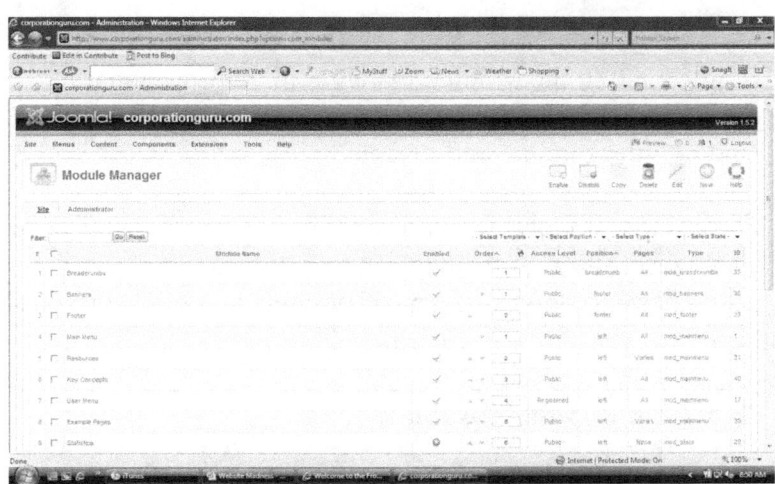

Now, click on your other internet screen and look at your website. Yours should look like this the next screen shot.

Do you see the module popular on your website?

We are going to disable this module.

Figure 25: Your website

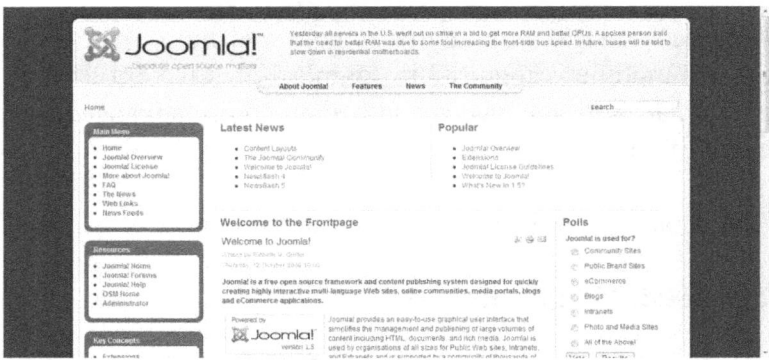

Toggle back to the Module manager in your dashboard.

Find popular module and disable it.

If you have noticed it is not on the first page. You need to scroll to the bottom of the page and click next.
Now check the box in front of popular and click the disable button.

Figure 26: Popular Disable

Now go back to your website and refresh the screen, if you see two blue arrows   heading in opposite direction this is refresh.

Did your popular module disappear? Now go back and re-enable it, refresh and relook at your website.

Try turning other modules on and off to see what happens. Don't forget to go back and forth to the first page and second page.

Figure 27: Popular Module gone

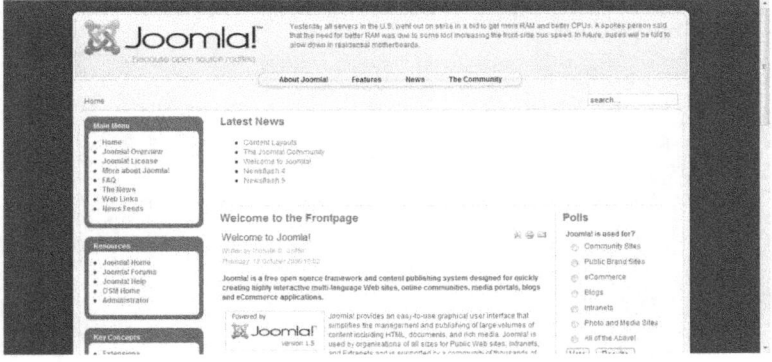

Module Manager- Changing

Now let's move module around a little bit. Let's go back to the module manager. Remember it is located under extensions/module manager. Now looking across the module manager there are a number of columns.

Figure 28: Module Manager Columns

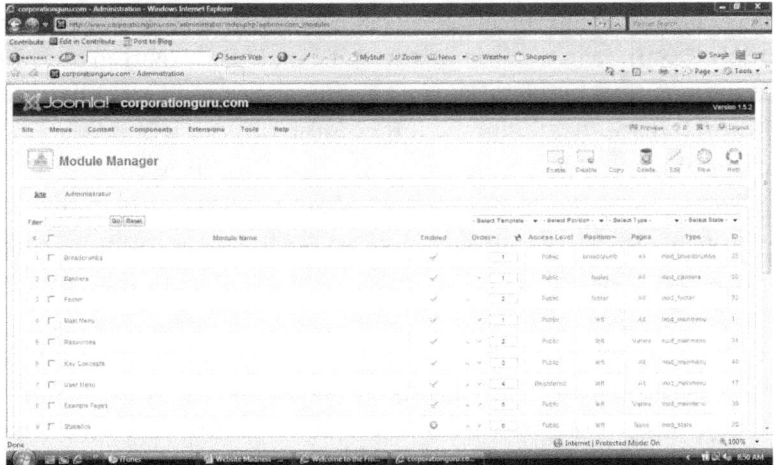

The columns are:

- # a number automatically assigned by Joomla

- Checkbox – Check this box to select an item and then click a command icon for instance disables or enable. There is a global checkbox on the column heading bar. If you check this box it selects everything on page. Go ahead and select the global check box and click disable. Now go back to your website, many of the modules have disappeared. Now go back and re-select the global and click enable go back to your website, the modules showed back up again.

- Module name – This is the name of the module. You can click on the name to open the module for editing. (You can also rename the modules when editing).

• Enabled – A green checkmark or a red circle with an X showing whether the module is enabled or disabled. Click the checkmark or red circle to enable or disable directly on the line. Go ahead and try it.

• Order – The order to display the modules. This means module 1 will be in the first position. Look at the position column; find the position labeled 'left'. This means that all modules with position left are located in the left column of your webpage. Look and see what module is number 1. It is "Main Menu" now go to your website and look at where Main menu is, it is in the first position in the left column. When you have multiple modules in the same position, you can order which comes first and which comes last.

• Access Level: Each module has security built around it, you can have modules which are Public and everyone can see them. You can have modules Registered, where only customers who are registered can view them. There is also, special these are users who have rights to change the website from the webpage. These are authors or editors of content for your website. Notice on your module screen the User Menu is registered, meaning only registered users will see this.

• Position: The position is where the module is displayed. We briefly covered in discussing the Order column. Positions are defined in template for the page.

• Pages: You can dedicate which modules show up on what pages based on the menu items.

• The type and Id are system identification and for this book, we will not be touching this area.

Now go to the bottom of the module page, there is a display button, showing 20. This means that 20 modules can be displayed at once. If you drop down the box, you see you can change it to any number of views. When you change the display let's say to 50, it stays as long as your current session is active. Once you log out it goes back to 20. I personally do not change this very often.

Back at the top of the module page there is a toolbar with icons, here are the descriptions:

• Enable   Enable – turns modules on. This button influences the enable column

• Disable Disable – turns modules off. This button influences the enable column.

At this point, the rest of the icons we will not using until latter. Therefore we will discuss then.

Let's move the modules around a little bit. Find the "Login Form" module. We will place with this one. If you toggle to your website, you find the Login Form is on the left side in the 4th position. But when you look at the Module Manager it is labeled 8th position.

Let's look at the screen in detail.

Figure 29: Module Manager – Login Form

Notice on the left column Main Menu is 1st, Resources is 2nd, Key Concepts is 3rd, User Menu is registered therefore does not count, Example Pages is 5th but really 4th on the website, Statistics is disable therefore does not count, and Login Form is 8th position but has moved to the 5th position on the website. But, wait a second. When you look at the website Login Form is in the 4th position.

Which one is missing?

Do you see that Example Pages is linked to Key Concepts? So now we want to move Login form to the 1st position. In order to edit a module we have to click on the module name for that module. Click on the underlined module name of Login Form.

Before we move the module positions, let's go through this form.
•Title: You can change this field to fit your needs. I like to

rename it to whatever type of website I am building. For instance, let say it is a Baseball site for a team called the Bandits. Then I would call it Bandits Login. This personalizes the website to your needs.

Figure 30: Module Form

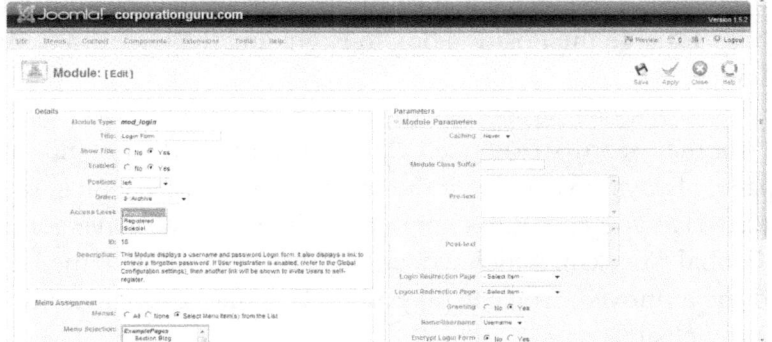

•   Show Title: This hides the title or shows it. On module's I show my custom titles but on Articles, I many times hide them. It is all personal preferences.

•   Enabled: Enables or Disables the module.

•   Position: This is all the positions the module can be placed in on your website. The positions are based on the template. The template defines the placement of modules on the page.

•   Order: This is what order the module will be placed based on the position. This was discussed in the Module Manager section.

•   Access level: This was discussed in the Module Manager section

•   Menus: All you to select what page the module will fall on. If you select "All" it is all pages in the website. If you select Menu Item from list, then based on the Menu Selection box, the pages will only show up in that place. Go back and look at Example Pages in the Module Manager. Notice how the menu only shows up on certain pages and on the front page it shows up under Key Concepts.

We will cover Parameters later in this book.

Now, let's go back and change the Login Module position to the right side, and put it in the first or second position after polls. Change the Position box to Right and the Order to 0:Main Menu.

Another word of advice, when in Joomla do not hit back space, always save and exit the screens through the icons. If you backspace you end up locking up modules and we have conduct a Global Check-in which we will discuss next. Notice the Login Form has moved. You can play around and move modules around your website.

Figure 31: Login Form Module moved to Right Side

Global Checkin

This is important to know and understand. When you exit a screen in Joomla it is best to Save or Cancel; pressing the back button causes some session to lock up. To test a session locking up do the following.

Go back into the Login Form we just discussed in the previous Chapter. Instead of hitting save or cancel, click the back button in Internet Explorer . This will cause the module manager to lock up. To unlock you can do one of two things. Go back into the module and exit it properly using Save or Cancel. Or use the Global Check-in.

The global check-in is found under on the toolbar under Tools/ Global Check-in. Do you see in the figure below, I have two sessions locked. They are showing with a checkmark. Just entering the session re-checks all sessions back in. Pretty simple and straight forward, but can be a nuisance if you work fast and a session locks on you. Therefore handy to know.

Figure 32: Global Check-in

File Manager

Before we get into the aesthetics and the articles of your website, we need to learn about files and permissions.

In order to access the file manager you will need to open your Cpanel again.

Go back to the Cpanel section, to review how to log in.

Figure 33: Cpanel

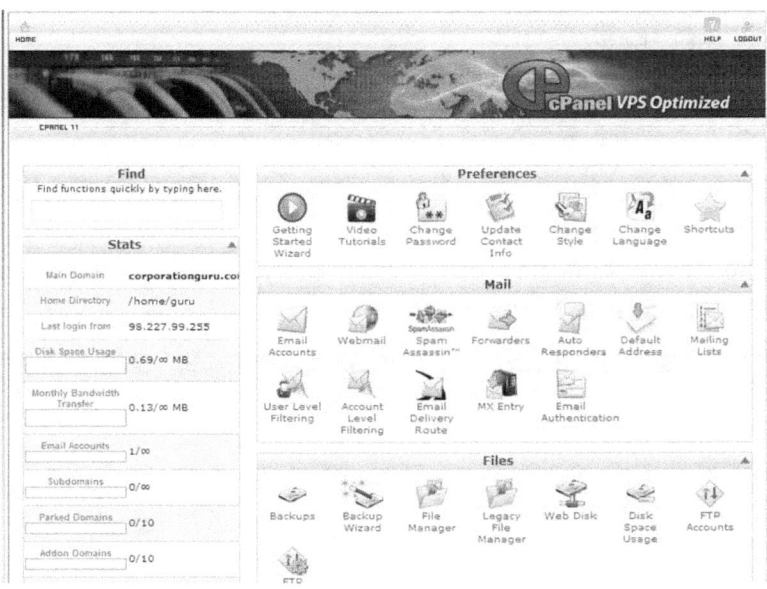

Under Files this is an icon labeled File Manager. Double click on this icon.

The following box opens up. Select Web Root and check the box for hidden files then press GO.

Figure 34: File Manager Selection

The view below show be what you see once you press GO.
Figure 35: File Manager View

Before we change anything, you need to learn about permissions. When you look to the far right column on the diagram on the previous page, you see numbers 777, 755, 644 these are permissions on the file. These numbers are critical to security of your site. You do not want people to screw up your website, because you left permissions open where anyone can access your files.

The first number means Owner permissions

The second number means Group permissions

The third number stands for World permissions (basically anyone anywhere)

Figure 36: File permissions

Within each number there are different numbers based on read, write or execute access. Permissions is defined in UNIX as:
- r- Read permission - is either a 4 or -
- w– Write permission – is either a 2 or -
- x- Execute permission – is either a 1 or –

For example if a permission is set at 777, this means the following:

Owner		Group World
rwx	rwx	rwx
421	421	421

Now, let's say the permissions are 755, this means the owner can do everything but group and world can read or write:

Owner		Group World
rwx	rwx	rwx
421	4-1	4-1

Another example, is 644, this is typically used for system files or folders:

Owner		Group World
rwx	rwx	rwx
42-	4--	4--

So now that you know about permissions, we need to modify a few file permissions and then once we are done with the files we need to change them back.

The first thing we have to do is rename the .htaccess file. If you notice it is only 0 bytes. This is a dummy file. We need to replace it with the htaccess.txt file which is the file the bots search for from the search engines. Without this file in place the search engines cannot find your website. This is the 1st step in any SEO optimization process.

We need to do is rename the .htaccess file to htaccess1.txt. You must remove the period in front of the htaccess file and then rename it. This file is renamed by clicking on the name in the file manager and click okay.

Second, we need to rename htaccess.txt to .htaccess. You must add the period in front of the htaccess and remove the .txt.

Your directly should look like this now.

Figure 37: htaccess file change

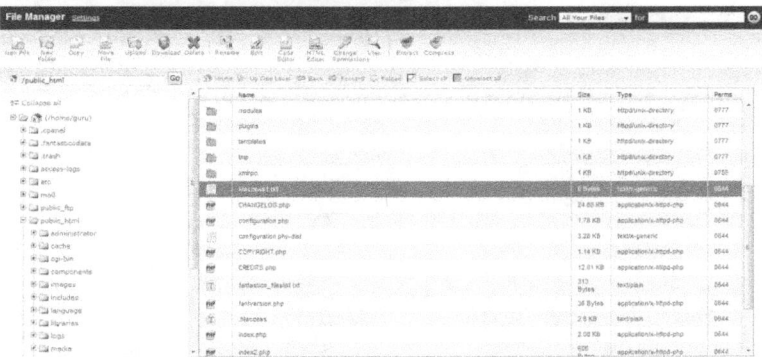

The item we need to change is the configuration.php file. This file controls the backend of Joomla and also allows your website to begin to increase its rankings when searched for on search engines. Notice this file is 644 permissions; we need to change it to 777. Make our changes in Joomla and then change it back to 644. This file is very critical; to security therefore do not forget to change it back.

Highlight the line for configuration.php. Now if you click to much there will be other lines highlighted. This is annoying. You will need to click off the other lines, make sure only the configuration.php line is highlighted. Then go to the tool bar on top and click on the change permission icon.

Change
Permissions

This pops up the following screen:

Figure 38: Change Permission screen

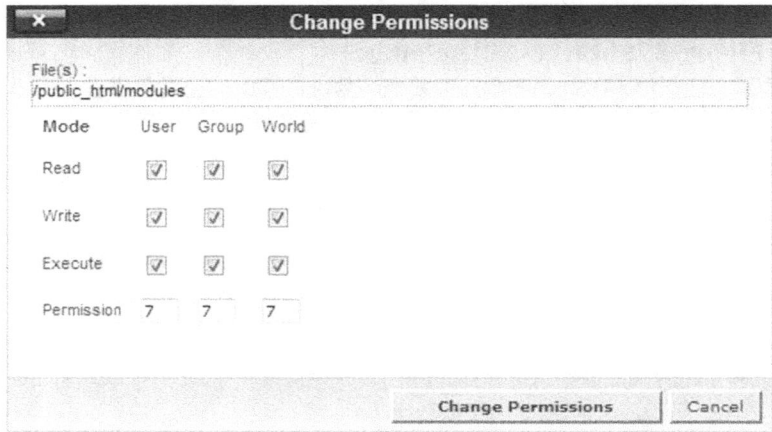

Change it to 777 by checking all the boxes. Click change permissions.

Okay, now let's go back into the Joomla dashboard; leave the cpanel open and the file manager. We will be coming right back to it. You will probably have to log back in.

Updating Global Configuration

When you are back at the main dashboard, go to the toolbar. The first selection on the toolbar is site. If you place your mouse over this a drop down menu appears and you need to select GLOBAL CONFIGURATION.

Figure 39: Configuration.php file

The first thing we are going to do is reset the SEO settings. In order to increase your site rankings you have to have friendly names and you must have .html show up as suffixes on your URL's (site address). This area is critical to your site rankings.

To do this right, you must follow these directions.

First under SEO Settings change the Search Engine Friendly URL's to YES then click the save icon. (DO NOT CHANGE ANYTHING ELSE).

This sends you back to the main dashboard. There should be a Blue line, which states the global configuration file was updated.

Figure 40: Global configuration Dashboard

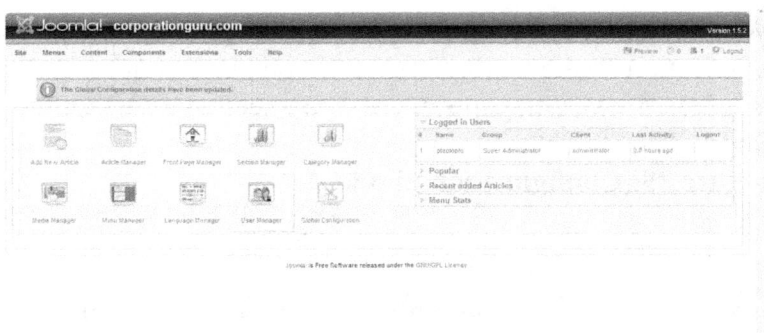

Go back into the Global Configuration file. Again it is under Site/ Global Configuration.

Now, we need to update the SEO Setting for Add Suffix to URL's. Change this to YES and click Save again.

Finally, go back into the Global Configuration again. Under SEO Setting change Apache Mod_rewrite to YES and click Save.

Now, the SEO section is done for now.

We want to go back into the Global Configuration file and we will update the meta data. Meta data is what search engine's use to show your site when a key word is used.

Under Global Site Meta Description, delete the text which is there and enter a description as to what your site does.

Then under Global Site Meta Keywords enter all the keywords someone would search for your site in the search engines. The words are separated by a comma. Do not use sentence only keywords. Below is how your configuration file should look. Do not change anything else at this time.

Figure 41: Global Configuration

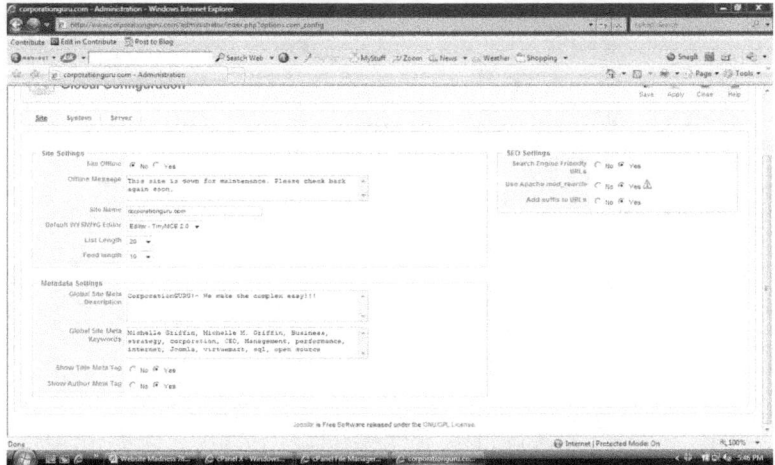

Now we need to go back and reset the permissions to 644 from 777.

Go back to your Cpanel screen File Manager.

You will need to refresh the screen or the Change Permission icon will not work.

Highlight the configuration.php file and click the change permissions icon on the toolbar.

Change the boxes to the following:

Figure 42: Permissions

Templates

Now that we fixed the Global configuration file, we will modify the template. In order to modify the standard template, we have to change the permissions of the file which manages the template.

First, lets go into the Joomla dashboard and look at the templates; on the dashboard toolbar go to Extensions/Template Manager. Joomla! 1.5 comes with 2 templates. But, you can subscribe to services where additional templates can be purchased. I subscribe to Rocket Themes. They have versatile templates and have never found an error in them. Plus they are always coming up with new stuff.

Figure 43: Template Manager

If you notice there are two templates pre-installed. Let's change the default template from rhuk_milkay to beez. You do this by clicking the circle in front of the template name and then clicking the default icon. Now go back to your website and refresh the page. You should not see the page has changed to the new template as shown in the figure.

Figure 44: Beez Template

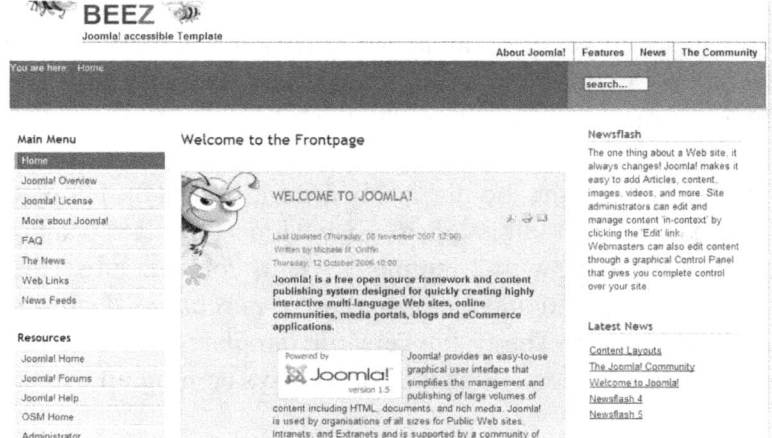

Now go back to your Joomla Dashboard and reset your template to the original template. Click on the circle in front of the template name and click Default. Refresh your website; it is back to the original look. Now let's begin to tweak the template. Click on the template name and it takes you to the configuration screen.

Figure 45: Milky way Template Configuration

Now there are a few modifications you can do with this site. If you look on the right hand side there is a Color Variation and Background Variation buttons. Just change the color and click save. Then go back to your website and refresh the screen to see the effect. If you noticed nothing changed. The reason why is because the file is unwritable. Go back to the Joomla Dashboard and back to the Template Manager.

Click on the Template name for rhuk_milkway; notice the right hand side above the color selection it says the params.ini file is unwritable; to change the colors than we need to change the permissions of the params.ini file.

Go to the Cpanel File Manager. The params.ini file is located in the Template folder, in the name of the template we are using which is rhuk_milkway. Open up the template folder and highlight the params.ini and change the permissions to 766. The changing of permissions was discussed in the previous chapter, if you forgot how to do this.

Figure 46: Params.ini file location

Go back to the Joomla Dashboard to the Template Manager (Extensions). Change the color again. Go to your website and refresh, and the new color appears.

Templates add a flavor to your website; it makes it personal and unique. This next step is to show you what a template looks like, how to load it and how it changes the look of your site. The template is from Rocket Theme (www.rockettheme.com).

A sidenote: There are 100's of Joomla modules you can download and use on your site. In order to keep them organized, I recommend keeping a Joomla folder or a download folder in your documents folder where all your modules and templates are stored on your computer.

Figure 47: Window Explorer IPOD as Extra Drive

If you have a hard drive which is pretty full, many people don't know their IPOD by Apple is an extra hard drive.

I have a 160 GB IPOD hook to my computer all the time and

store all my files on it, versus my laptop.

If you want to see how the IPOD works go to Windows Explorer or My computer, you will notice your IPOD as the G: drive.

I actually keep all my files on my IPOD then when I travel to a customer site, I can hook up to any computer if I don't want to pull out my laptop. I will show you how to download modules in the next chapter.

Side Note: This book is based on the latest version of Joomla 1.5. Do not load Joomla 1.0 Legacy, even though it says compatible I have found issues.

To install Templates you go to Extensions on the toolbar in your Joomla Dashboard; select Install/Uninstall.

Note, you go to the same place to install new templates, modules, and components are pretty straight forward.

Figure 48: Install Template

Browse for your template file. It will have the extension .tgz extension (this is a Unix file).

If the template or modules installed correctly the following screen will appear.

Figure 49: Template Success

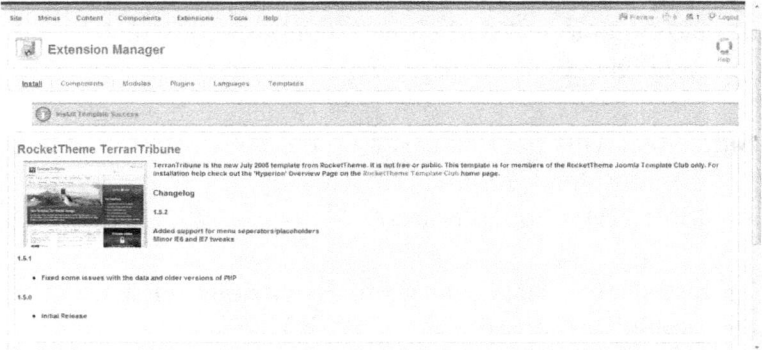

In order to change the template we have to go back to the Template Manager, under Extensions/Template Manager.

We then are going to change the template to Default. We learned this at the beginning of this chapter.

The next screen shot shows how a template can change the look of your website dramatically.

We will show you how to build this site at the end of the book. But, for right now we will stay on the basics.

Figure 50: New Template Example

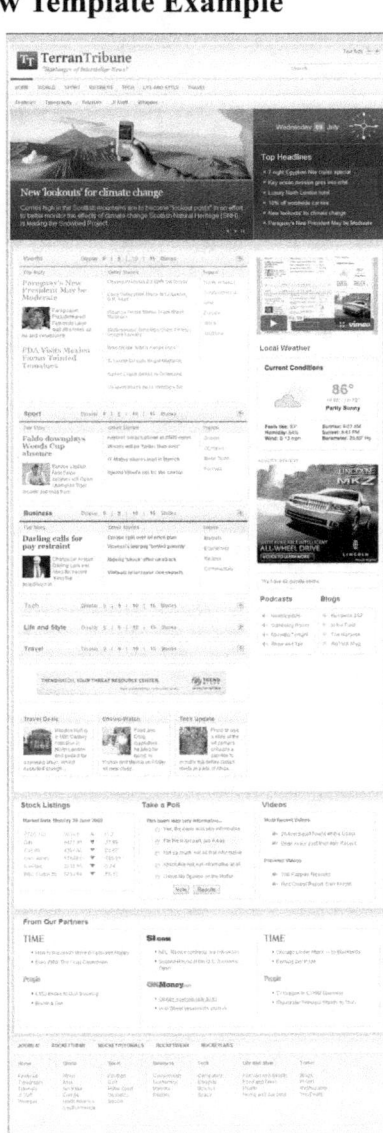

Articles

We are now going to begin customizing the website with our own content. To change and add article content is located on the toolbar under Content/Article Manager.

Figure 51: Article Manager

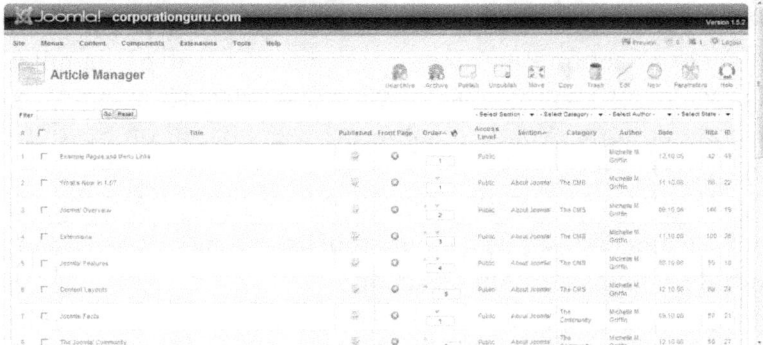

The functionality is pretty cool. There is a lot of functionality here so we will start with the basics, many of the columns functionality are the same as the Module Manager which we covered in a previous chapter.

• Checkbox- is used to activate an icon on the top of the screen, let's say publish or unpublish.

• Title- is the name of the article.

• Published- has a checkmark if published or a red circle with an x if not published.

• Front page – This is content which appears on the front page. If this is unchecked it will not appear on the front page of your website.

• Order – is the position of the article compared to other articles, which come at the top of the website.

• Access Level – is public or registered. Registered means they must have an account and be logged in.

• Section – These are defined by you. Each article must belong to a Section and Category. Security can also be applied to this, where let's say you are hosting a sports page and you have different editors. You can authorize users based on Sections to edit.

• Category – goes along with sections.   There can be multiple categories within a section.

• Author – Who created and edited the article.

• Date- The date last edited

• Hits – How many people read the article.
ICONS

• Unarchive – put a file archived back into production

• Archive – place file in archive mode (when Archived the article is still there just grayed out, must be unarchived before it can be edited again.

• Publish – Show article on website

• Unpublish – Hide article from website

• Move – Select new Category for article

• Copy – Select article and copies existing article, marks it unpublished. Need to Change name and republish.

• Trash – sends articles to trash (does not really delete them until you go to Trash and finally delete them.

• Edit – Edit article, you can also click on the title to Edit.
• New – Create new article.

• Parameters- change global article settings.

Figure 52: Article Parameters

The parameters I change are the following; it is personal preference if you change them.
• Author Name – Hide
• Created Date and Time - Hide
• Modified Date and Time – Hide

You can play around with the parameters as you build your site, to determine what you want on or off.

Edit an Article

Since the sample Joomla data was loaded there are a load of articles to edit or we can create new. If you look at your website the main article is Welcome to Joomla, do you see it in the middle of the screen shot below. This article we need to find in the article manager. It is located on the second page with a section of NEWS.

If you don't want to search through the documents, if you knew the section was news you can filter the articles by looking up only Sections. Just below the icons there are filters. If you drop down the Select Section box, and pick NEWS it will show you only that section. Just remember once you turn on a filter the filter stays on until you log out.

Figure 53: Welcome to Joomla

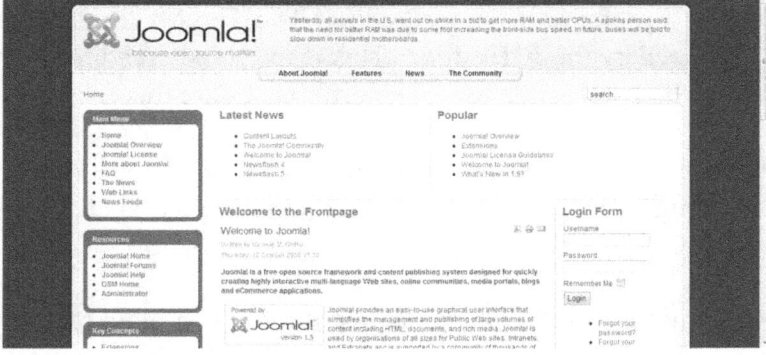

Also notice on the website front page, do you see the Author name and edit time, depending on the site, I am creating I hide this in the parameters screen as discussed above.

Let's click on the Welcome to Joomla article and look at the edit page.

This page, you notice has an image, as well as different bolded text. We need to add our own personal text in there. But first let's look at the editor.

Figure 54: Welcome to Joomla Article

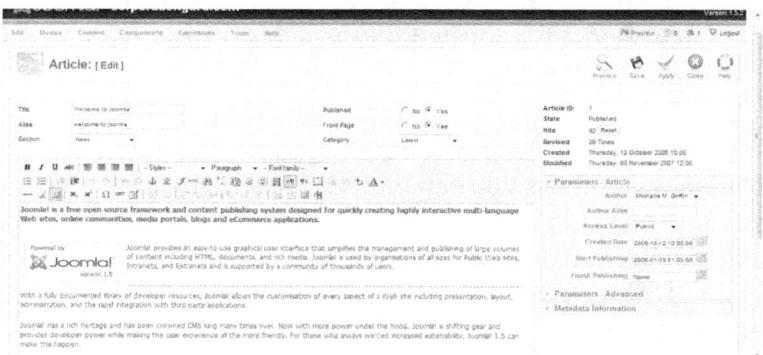

I myself prefer an enhanced editor. The TinyMCE editor can be enhanced by the JCE editor. This is the standard editor many people who use Joomla use. The differences are this

·

•   if you drop down the Paragraph selector it shows Heading 1, Heading 2, Heading 3 but does not show you what it looks like.

•   Under font family, it just list the fonts in plain text with the JCE Editor it enhances it showing what the fonts look like. There are also additional plugins which make the editor feel like a traditional word processor.

This is just a few differences, so I will walk you through the fields on this page. But then we will edit the article in the next chapter, after we install the JCE editor component.

The important features of the article screen are the following:
- Title – name of article, this will appear on the website.

- Alias – This needs to be a single word or multiple words tied together with a dash or underscore. This is used by the search engines to index your page. Therefore try to keep it simple but descriptive.

- Section – is the area this article belongs to. Every article must have a section and category

- Category – which category within the section does it belong.

- Published – Yes or No

- Front Page – Yes or No

Over on the Right there is Article Parameters, these are only changed if you want to. Otherwise they will use the global settings discussed earlier in this chapter.

The most important thing is the Meta Description and Meta Keywords. Remember we did it for the Global Configuration.

This is important to fill out; this will be found by the search engine robots. The more key information the higher you website will appear.

Just realize no matter what you do it takes 3 to 6 months for your website to move up the ranks. The more it is searched the better. If you made changes then save or if you have not then exit. Let's learn how to install the JCE editor

Loading an Editor Component

If you are like me, you like to have an editor which is "What you see is What you get" (WYSIWYG).

There is an editor which comes with Joomla, it is called Tiny MCE is a WYSIWYG, but I change it to JCE Editor. You can use the Tiny editor or I will walk you through on how to install the JCE editor.

Step 1: Go to www.joomla.com (A good idea to register on this site, so you can look at the forums).

Step 2: On the toolbar on the Joomla website click Extensions (Now, don't get to excited there are 3,000 extensions, some are Non-Commercial (free) and some you pay for Commercial. You will learn how to download, and then you can experiment me on your site, after it is built. Just try to stay with Native 1.5 modules.

Figure 55: JCE Reviews

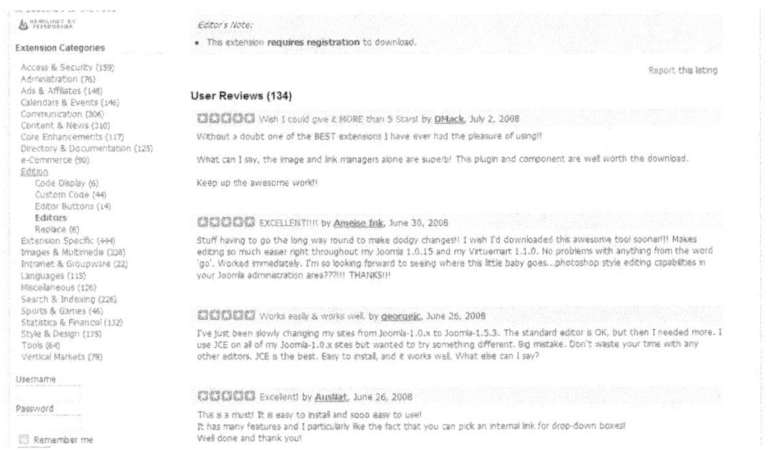

Step 3: You can search on this site for editors or scroll down to Edition/Editors and click on this link.

Step 4: Look for JCE – Note: when ever looking for a new module or component, look at the reviews. I have downloaded a few modules which break the site. I try to stay with stable versions which others have written about. Click on the Reviews link to see the reviews.

Scroll up the page, and press download. This will open a new screen. Which is the JCE homepage, some sites if you are downloading would like you to register.

Figure 56: JCE Download

Downloads Home   Search Document

Categories

Files

JCE Utilities   4
JCE Utilities and other Extras

JCE Language Packs   12
Language Packs for JCE

JCE 3PD Plugins   0
3rd Party Plugins for JCE

These are unofficial JCE plugins contributed by JCE users.

JCE Plugins   12
Official Optional Plugins for JCE

JCE Editor Mambot / Plugin   6
JCE Editor Mambot / Plugin

JCE Admin Component   5
Required Admin Component for JCE 1.1.x and 1.5.x

Side Note: There are different versions of modules and components. My recommendation is only use RC1 or above on your website. This is an officially released version. The releases follow the following:

• Beta 1 – Major revision or new module or component – Not PRODUCTION ready

• Beta 2 – Better than Beta 1 – NOT PRODUCTION READY

• Beta 3 & 4 – some modules may not go through this stage. This means still NOT PRODUCTION READY

• RC1 - Release Candidate 1 – means initial Production Ready (this means it can be used in production site, but there may be bugs.)

• RC2-RC4 – Enhanced released candidates- usually minor stuff being fixed. Usually when it passes RC2 – I will use it knowing it could break something or have bugs.

• Production – Is officially Production Ready – and ready for mass public use. Of course, there could still be bugs, which are never found until a lot of people are using it.

Now that you are on the JCE page, we are looking for the JCE Admin Component. Click on the link. It brings us to the download page.

We need the JCE Admin Component for Joomla 1.5. Click on this link it brings you to the download page.

Figure 57: JCE download for Joomla! 1.5:

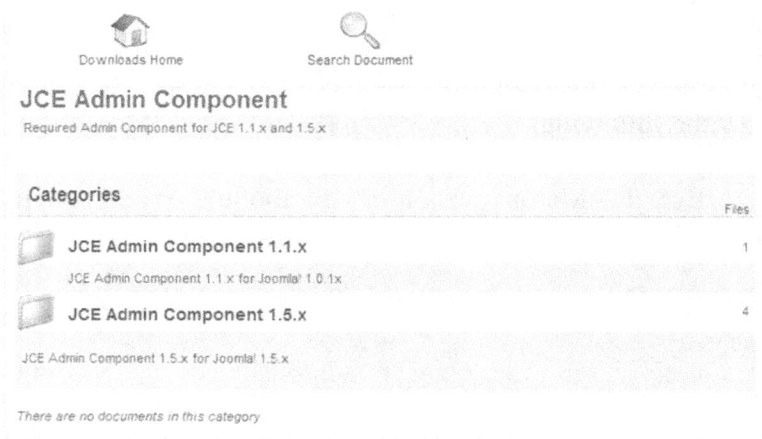

Click on JCE Administration component 1.5.0 the link has a yellow open box in front of it, see Figure 45.

Figure 58: Saving a file

This pops up a box to run or save. You need to save it on your computer in the folder you created for Joomla files.

I recommend you create a subfolder for it also.

When the screen shows to save file, on the right side search for your folder where you are saving your Joomla files. Click new folder, name it the name of the download (JCE) and save the file to this folder.

Figure 59: Download JCE

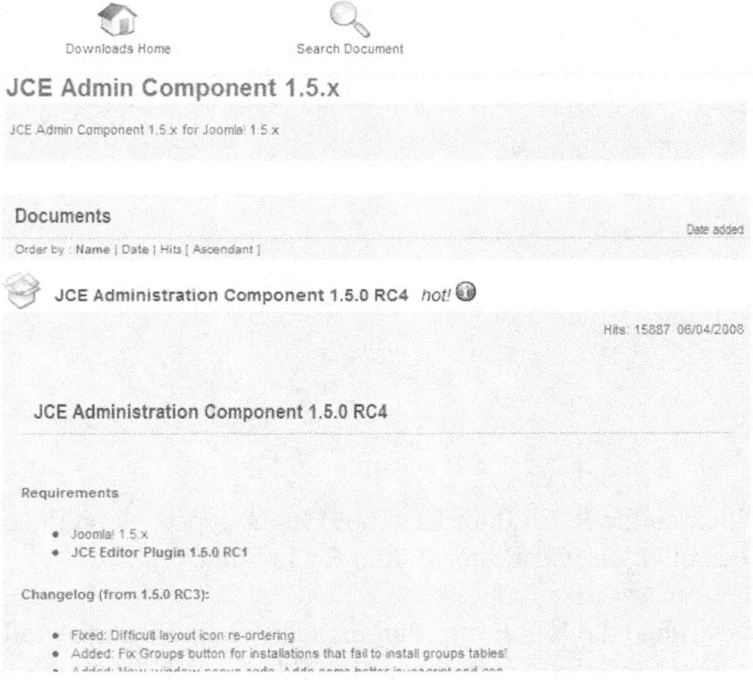

Before we leave we also need the Editor plug-in, which is required. Therefore use the back button on your Internet Explorer to go back a few screens. We want to be back on the following page.

Figure 60: JCE Main Screen

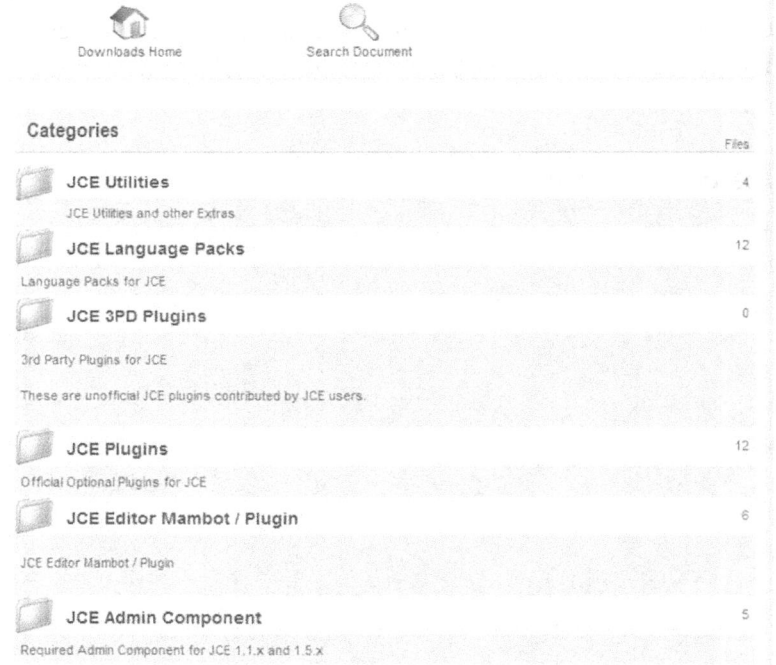

Click on the JCE Editor Mambot/Plugin hyperlink on the next screen click on JCE Editor Plugin for Joomla! 1.5.

Download the JCE Editor Plugin the hyperlink with the yellow box next to it. Save it in the same folder as you saved the JCE Admin component.

Now, we close out of the Joomla website and JCE. Let's install the editor. Go back into your Joomla Dashboard; you may need to log in. Now we are going to install the JCE component. To do this, it is the same way install Templates. Go to Extensions Install/Uninstall.

Put your cursor in the Package Name field and browse for the file on your computer. Then click upload and install.

Figure 61: Install JCE

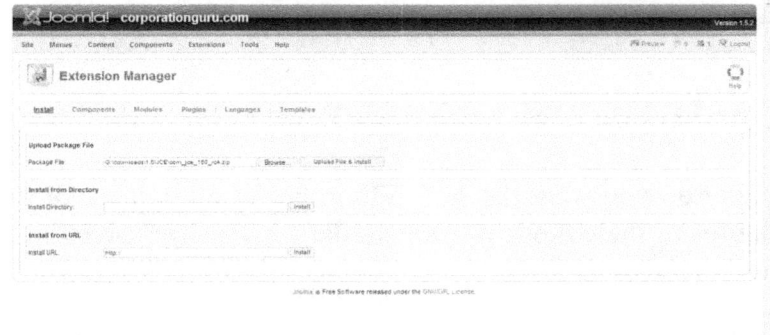

Scroll to the bottom of the install page, once the JCE Admin component successfully installs and browse for the JCE Editor plug-in. Click Upload file and install.

Now that we have changed the editor, we now need to update the editor in the User Manager or Global configuration. If you want to update in the Global Configuration then refer back to the Global Configuration chapter. You will need to go in and change the permissions in File Manager for the configuration.php file to 777. Then go to Joomla and update the file. Don't forget to go back and reset the permissions to 644, when you are through.

To update in the User Manager, go to Site/User Manager. Click on your name.   On the User Manager Detail sheet, change the User Editor to JCE.

Figure 62: User Manager

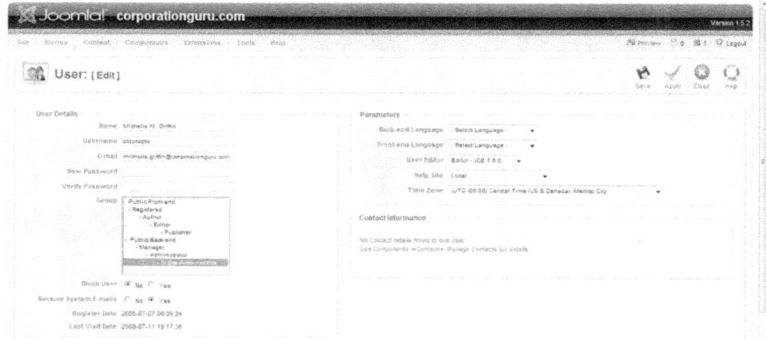

Why do you want the JCE Editor, because it adds additional features to the editor to make similar to what we use today for word processing.

Let's go back into the article manager and edit the Welcome to Joomla article.

Open the article up by clicking on the article title.

Then drop down the box for Format. If you remember under the other editor, it just said, paragraph, header1, header 2.

Now with JCE installed, it shows what each will look like, if you selected header 1, header 2, etc...

If you look under Font, it now shows you what the fonts and font size will look like.

There are additional features, and you can also go out to the JCE website and download additional tool bars for additional WYSIWYG functionality.

Figure 63: JCE Editor Format

Article Section Manager

Now that we have discussed the Article Manager and modified articles; we need to ensure that we have Sections setup in order for us to control where articles are published and on what page.

The Section Manager is located in the Joomla Dashboard under Content/Section Manager on the top navigational bar.

Sections are top level folders, where as Categories are sub-folders within the top level Folder.

Let's go in and change the Section names which are the defaults installed with Joomla.

Figure 64: Section Manager

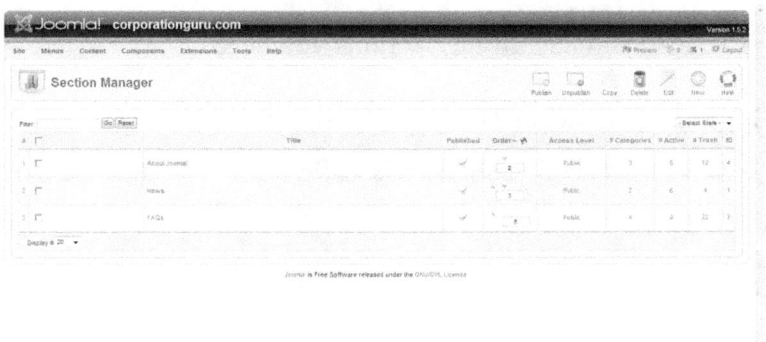

As you can see there are 3 default sections. Given I am creating a soccer website, I am going to name them Soccer Corner, Soccer News and Soccer FAQs. You can change yours to whatever you want to fit your site.

We can either modify the existing section which are there or delete them and create new ones. I am just going to modify them. To do this, just click the Title and it brings you to the Section Detail page, where I am going to change the Title and add a description. When finished click Save.

Figure 65: Section Detail

Go ahead and add all the sections you need.

Figure 66: Section Manager Updated

Article Category Manager

A Category is a sub-item of a Section. There can be multiple categories within a section.

The category manager is accessed via Content/Category Manager.

Figure 67: Category Manager

As with the section manager, you can either modify the default categories or delete them. If you look under Section you can see what section the category is tied to.

Go ahead and make changes to the Categories.

Note, it will not let you delete a category or a section if there is content still attached, meaning there is an article. You will need to go into the Article Manager and change the Section and Category if you want to delete them.

Let's edit the categories.

Figure 68: Category Detail

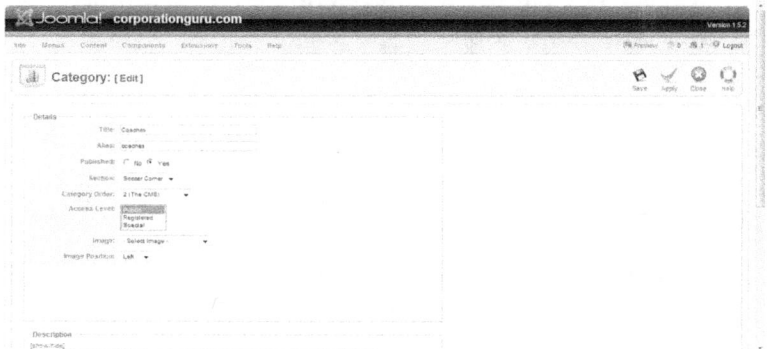

I am changing all of them to fit the soccer theme, I have created. Change yours to fit your site.

Figure 69: Category Manager Changed

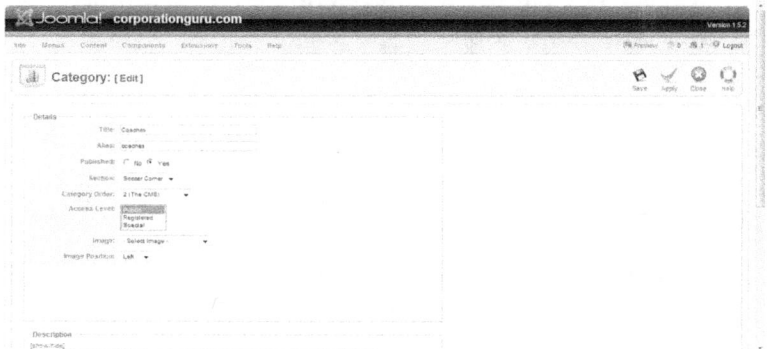

Article Trash

In order to delete a Section or Category, there cannot be any article tied to it.

Even articles that have been deleted in the Article Manager are not really deleted. They are sent to the Article Trash.

Therefore you must go to the Article Trash to cleanup the deleted articles. The article trash is located in Contents/Article Trash. I have deleted a number of excess articles, in which we modified back in the article section.

Figure 70: Article Trash

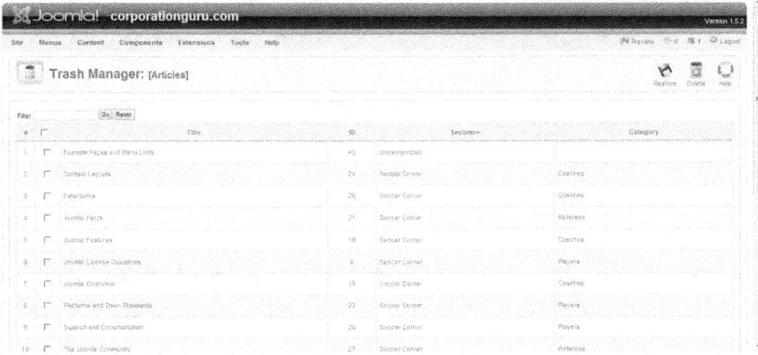

In my case, I am not going to be using the category Fees, which I created in the last chapter. Therefore I am going to delete it. But first I am going to delete all the articles in the trash, since they are generic to Joomla and I will not be using them.

Special note: You should read many of the articles, because it adds additional help on how to do certain topics in Joomla, which I may have missed in this book.

First check all the articles tied to the category or section you will be deleting. A category must be deleted before a section. Then once all categories are deleted then the actual section can be deleted.

Also, if you accidently deleted a document from the Article Manager, you can check the box in front of the document and click the Restore icon at the top of the screen.

Figure 71: Permanently delete

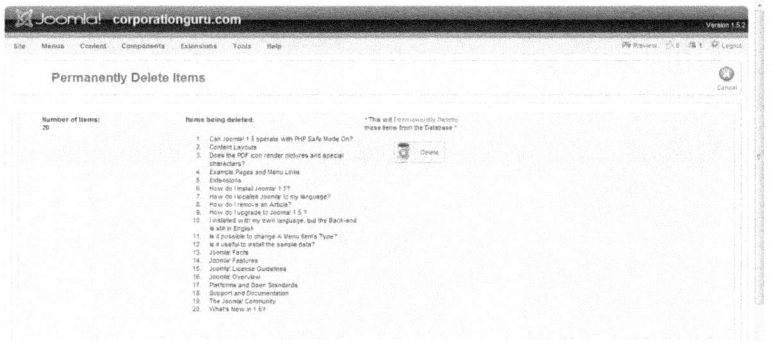

Select the documents you want to delete and press the Delete Icon. Then the permanently delete screen appears press the Delete button.

Now go back to your Category Manager, and check the category you wish to delete. Press delete. If it does not delete, it means there are still articles tied to it. You will need to go back to the Article Manager and Trash to find out what is tied to the category.

Editing a Front Page Article

Let's go out and officially edit the Welcome to Joomla Front Page article. I am going to build a Soccer website as part of the initial tutorial. You can build the same or create whatever site you would like. Remember it is easy to change, once you go through the tutorial the first time and then go back and re-create your site your way.

Open up the Welcome to Joomla Front Page article.
Step 1: Change the title to Soccer News
Step 2: Change alias to Soccer_news
Step 3: Leave Category and Section for now.
Step 4: Delete the Joomla Text
Step 5: You can write your content in word processor and paste it into the document or you can type your paragraph. Let's save and go out to or website and see how it looks.

Figure 72: Soccer News

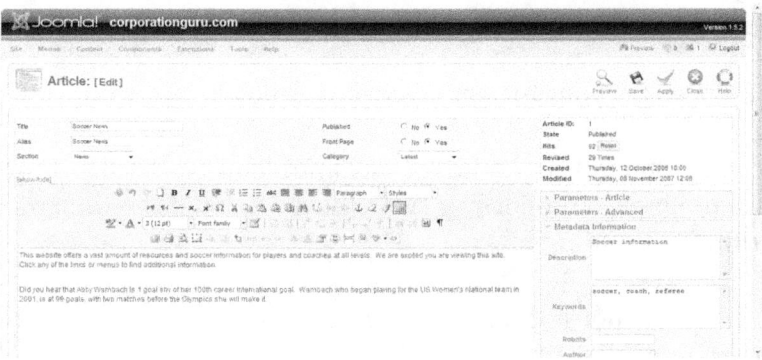

Now that you have changed this article, let's add a picture to it. Go out the internet and find a picture you would like to upload. It needs to be a jpg, gif or png file. I am going to look on the internet for a soccer ball.

I am going to go to www.google.com and type in soccer ball jpg png in the search field. I found some cut clipart files at www. clipartguide.com.

To save to your computer, right click the image and click save as. Browse to the folder you save your Joomla files then save.

Let's add your image to your article, we created in this section. At the bottom of your article there is an image button.

Before you click it, put your cursor where you would like the image added. I am going to add mine to the first line of the article in the center.

Therefore I am going to hit enter at the first line to add a line above the first line. Then click the center button.

Then you go to the bottom of the article and click image. This pops up an image box.

Browse for your file and click start upload.

Now sometimes, the image does not load on the first time. I assume this is a minor bug, which isn't fixed at the time of this writing.

If it does not appear with the other icons, just click browse again, find your file and click start upload. It should be there now.

Figure 73: Adding an article image

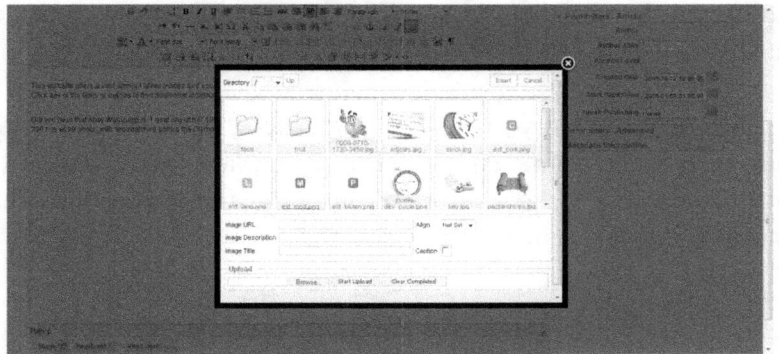

I have never had to upload an image more than twice. Once the image appears, click on it then click Insert. Your image should be in your article, now click save. Refresh your website and look at your new article.

Figure 74: Website

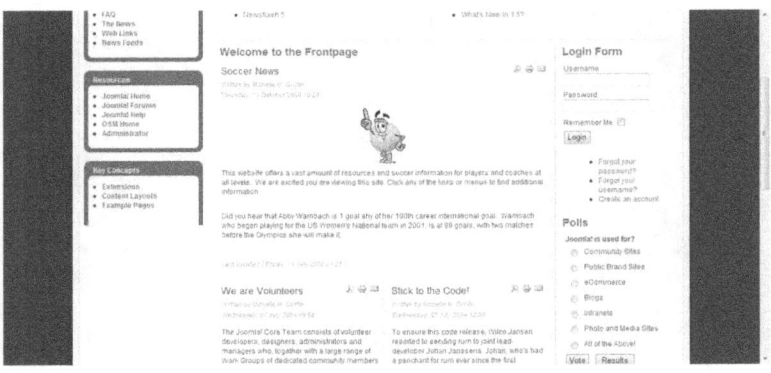

Now that you know how to change articles, any articles with the section NEWS are appearing on this front page, either edit the articles or unpublish them, to further customize your website.

Look through the other articles on the front page, if you are not going to use them then unpublish them or send them to trash, do this for all sections.

Side Note: When you have a long article, click the read more button at the bottom. This will break your article, where only a little content will show on the Front Page and if you click read more, it will take you to a new screen.

Polls

Your website is coming along with your own content. Let's modify the polls to be a survey based on our website. My poll is going to be about "What is your favorite sport?"

To do this, you need to go to Components/Polls.
Step 1: Click the Joomla Poll under Poll Title
Figure 75: Poll Manager

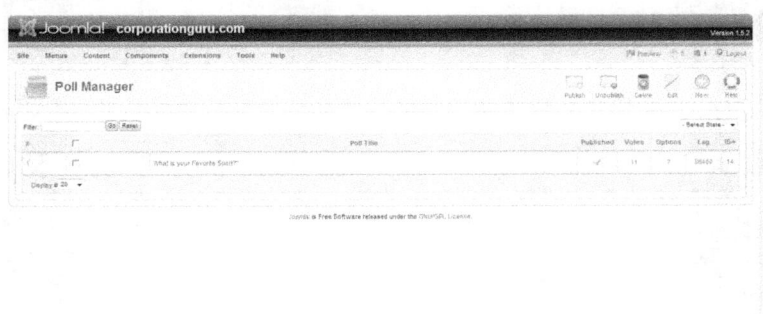

Step 2: Rename the title - mine is "What is your favorite sport?"
Figure 76: Poll Detail

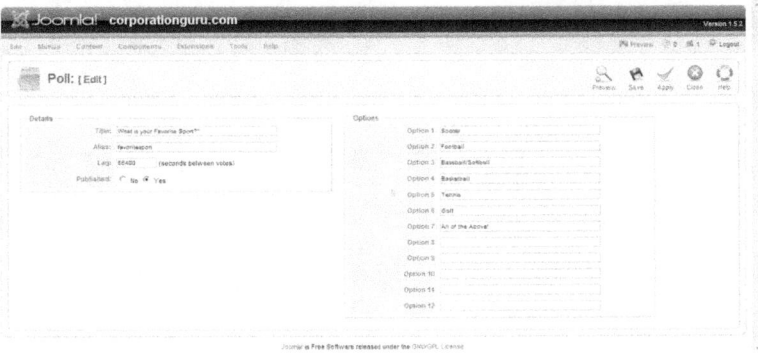

Step 3: Rename the alias; I am calling mine – sport

Step 4: Replace the options on the right hand of the screen and click save.

Refresh your website, how does your poll look?

Figure 77: Poll changed

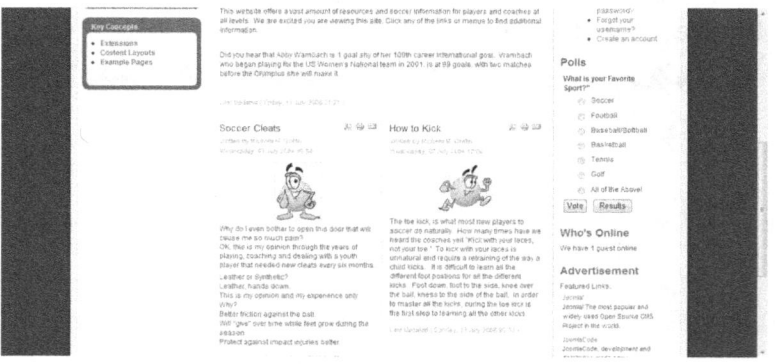

Menu Manager Overview

Since we have customized the articles, let's now customize the menus. The first thing we need to do is change the "Welcome to the Front Page" statement, to something which fits our site. To change this statement we need to go to Menu on the Joomla Dashboard.

There are different types of menus
- Main menu – which is the main navigational menu on all pages
- User menu – which is setup for registered users to see special areas
- Top menu – special navigation or articles for people to go to.
- Custom Menu – you can create your own menu

Let's go through the columns on the Menu Manager screen. To access the Menu Manager go to Menu/menu manager.

Figure 78: Menu Manager

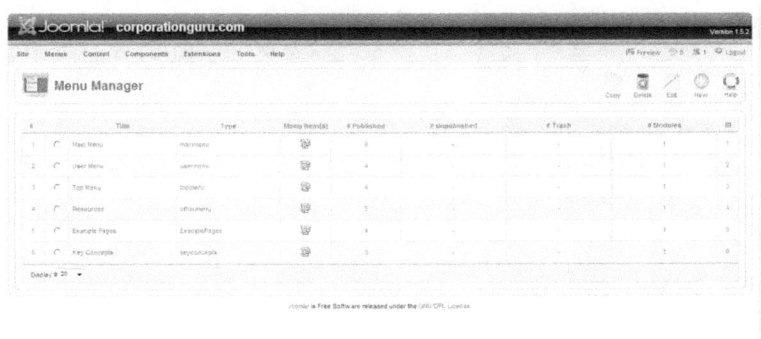

The columns are the following:
- # is the unique identifier of the menu, notice there are 6 menus. You can create as many menus as you would like.

• Title: is the name of the menu. To change the name just click the menu name.

• Type: is the type of menu this needs to be one word with no spaces

• Menu Items – allows you to edit the menu

• # Published – The number of menu items within this menu.

• # Unpublished – The number of menu items which are unpublished.

• # Trash – The number of menu items in trash

• # Modules – Modules tied to the menu. Main menus are article based, this tracks how many modules are tied to the menu.

• Id – a unique identifier

Let's click on the Menu Items and look at the detail menu screen for sub menu items.

Figure 79: Menu Item details

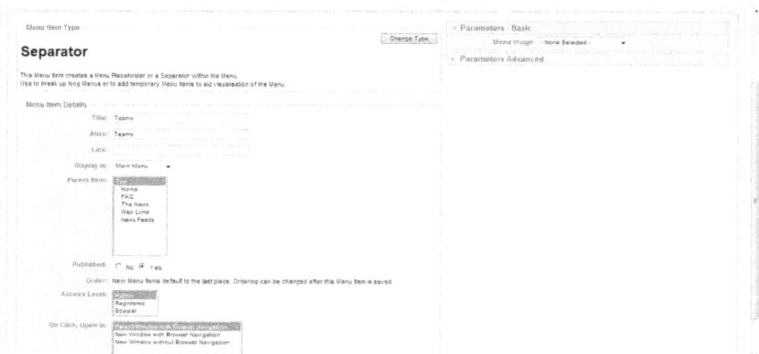

Note: Short cuts, instead of using the menu manager just go directly to the menu under the Menu dropdown.

Let's go to the main menu first, to change the "Welcome to the Front Page". Go to menu/main menu.

Figure 80: Main Menu

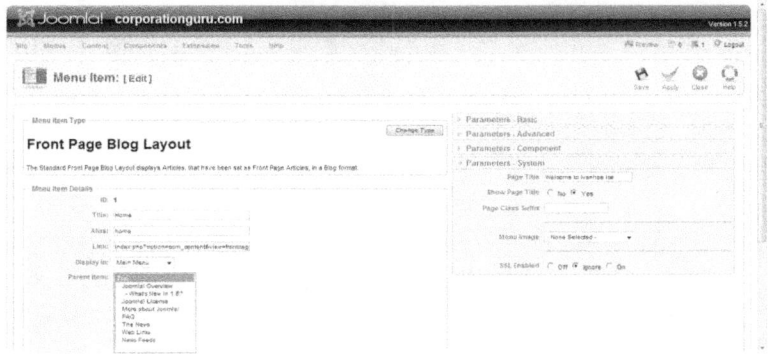

Let's double click on the menu item "Home".   On the right hand side there is the drop down arrows. The arrow we need to select is "system".

You will see the page title. Change this to something appropriate for your website.

Figure 81: Home Menu Parameters

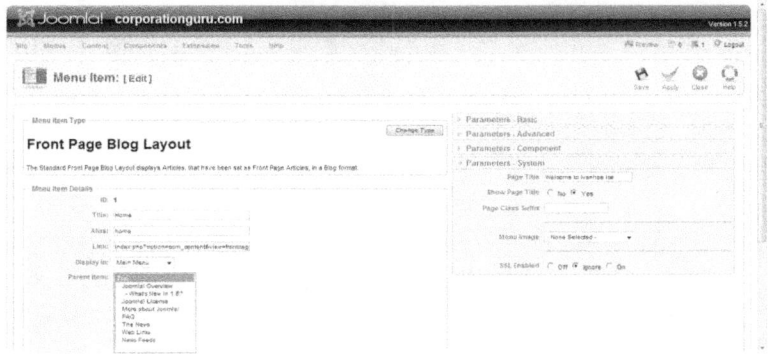

Since, I am building a sports site, I am going to type: "Welcome to Ivanhoe Ice", which is a local soccer team.

After you change it, click the save icon. Now, refresh your website.

Your website should now show your new title.

Figure 82: Website changed to Ivanhoe Ice

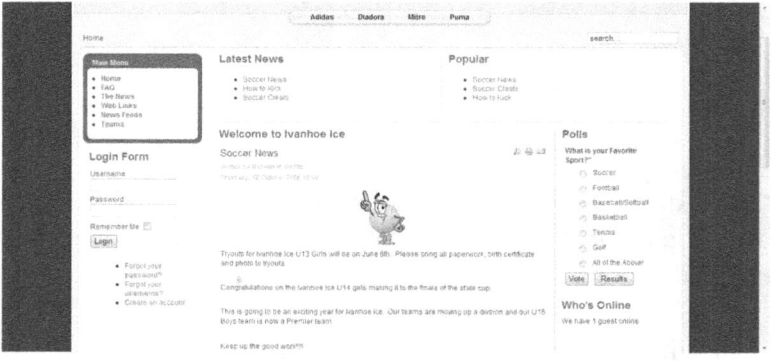

Modify Main Menu

Let's start modifying the links on the main menu. This is the module box in the left hand column.

Figure 83: Website

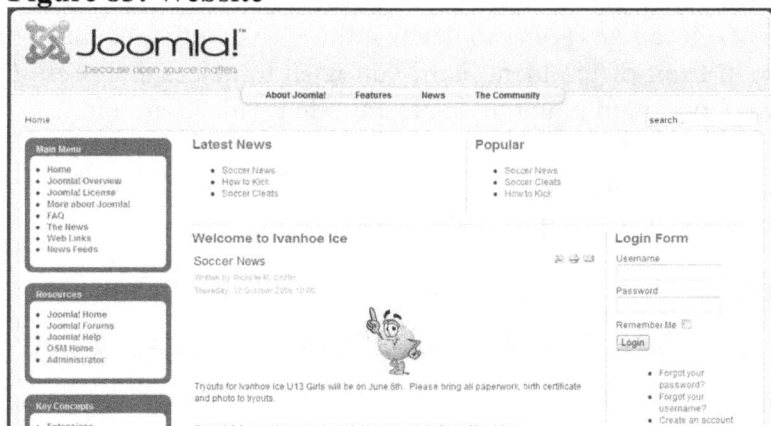

To do this we need to go to the Joomla Dashboard and highlight the menu toolbar. Before we went to Menu Manager this time we are going to go directly to the Main Menu.

Figure 84: Main Menu

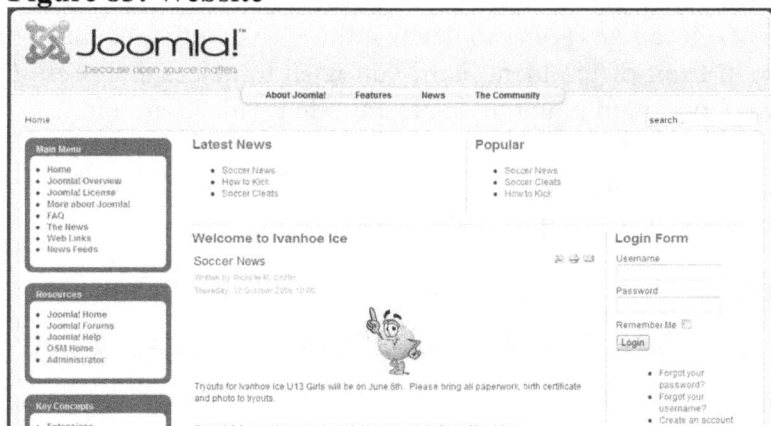

The Main Menu is your main menu. There must be at least 1 menu published within Joomla.

We can either trash the menu items which are there or modify them. In the case with the soccer website, I wish to set up teams,

Therefore I am going to delete a few. To delete you check the box in front of the menu item you wish to delete and press the trash icon. I am going to delete anything with Joomla in it.

Let's setup a new menu item called Teams. Click the New Icon. The following page pops –up

Figure 85: New Menu Item

When creating a new menu item, there are many selections to choose from; below is a summation of the types of menus.

•   Articles: This links to articles (Most used menu item)

•   Contacts – this displays all contacts or a single contact

•   Components – JCE Administration is a component, components can be setup as menu item if for instance you have someone else maintaining them or to access them the component it is through the menu. We will learn more about this when we install more components.

• News Feed – uses the component Newsfeed categories or it can display a single newsfeed.

• Poll – shows the component polls which we already have setup as a module. But if you had multiple polls this comes in handy as a menu item.

• Search – allows you to put a search link on your menu

• User – shows a list of users or a single user

• Weblinks – shows the Component Weblink which can be selected via categories or a single link.

• Wrapper – A wrapper allows you to have a link to an outside website but the frame is your site. The advantage to Wrappers is the viewer or customer never leaves your site, which means they come back to your site when finished. I use wrappers quite a bit.

• External Link – is similar to a wrapper, but they leave your site with no way back unless they hit the back button or re-type your site name.

• Separator – is placeholder for sub menu items

• Alias – An alias allows you to bring up similar content under a different name. Let's say you are running a blog. It allows you to have multiple blogs with different names.

Now, that we know the different types of menu items. We are going to create a menu item named Team. Since team is a separator of other categories for instance Boys teams and Girls teams we are going to select this.

Click New Icon to create a new menu item. Then let's click separator.

Figure 86: Menu Item Detail

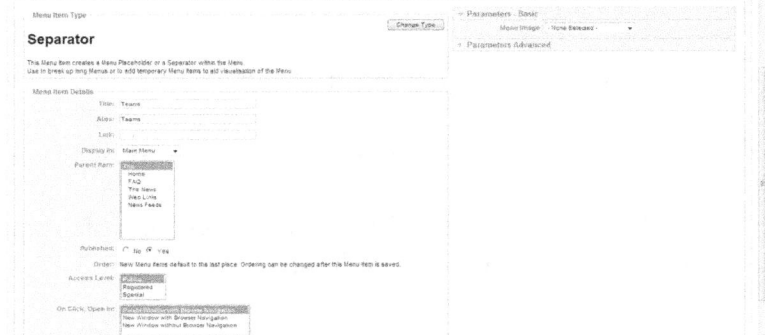

•   Enter your title for you new menu
•   Enter your alias (remember one word)
•   Parent Item: You can link this item below another item as a submenu. If it is a main menu item then leave it Top
•   Published – Yes or No
•   Access Level – Is it open to the public or registered
•   On Click, Open to: When your menu is clicked you can have it Open within the main winder or open a whole new browser. Browser navigation means you can hit the back arrow key to go back to the previous site.
If for someone reason you decide this was not the menu type you wanted to create, there is a change type icon at the top of the screen across from the name of the menu.

Weblinks

Joomla is nice because you can setup Weblinks easily to your favorite sites. Weblinks are good, because it gives you more exposure within the search engines.

The first thing we need to do is go to our Joomla Dashboard and click on Component/Weblinks/Links.

Figure 87: Weblinks

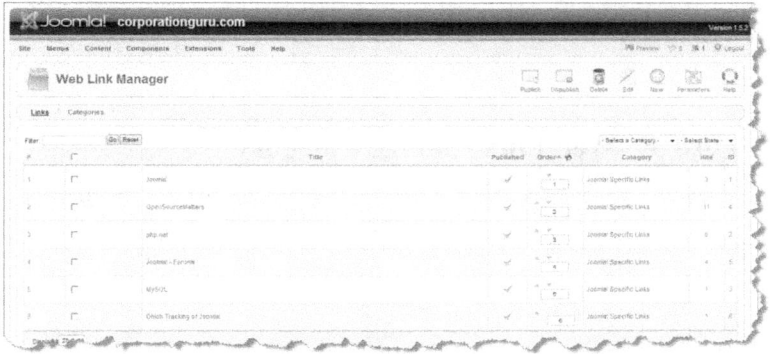

You should notice this screen looks the same as the other screens we have discussed.

If you notice there are two pages to Weblinks, Links and Categories. This is listed just under the Weblink manager name. Let's click on categories first and change the categories to what is appropriate for our site.

I am going to label my categories, soccer skills and coaching. Go ahead and click on the Category title and change the title, alias, description and add an image if you want.

Figure 88: Web Link Categories

Figure 89: Web Link Change Category

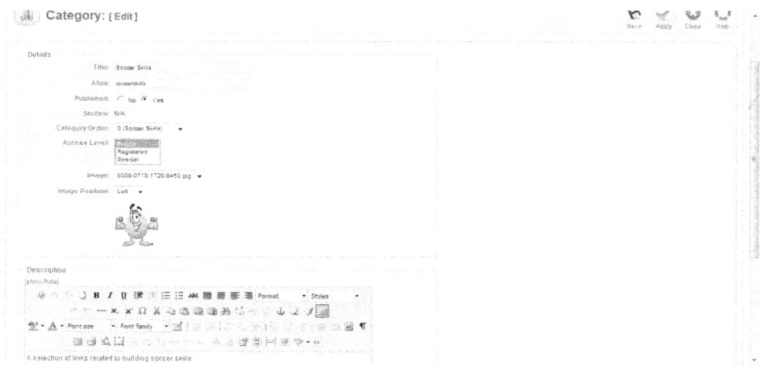

Now that we have changed the categories, let's now change the actual links. You will need the address of the websites you will like to have your site visitors' link to. The address looks like this:

http://www.corporationguru.com

Given our example is a soccer website; I will make all the links soccer based. This is what mine looks like below.

Figure 90: Weblinks Soccer

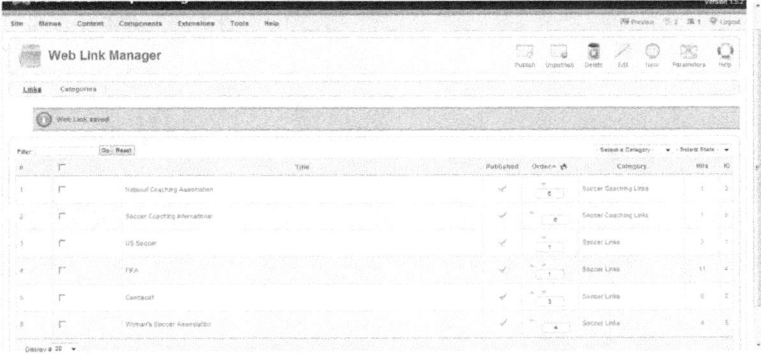

Now, refresh your site, under Weblinks on the main menu will show your new links.

Wrappers

Wrappers are my favorite, I use them extensively because I want to be able to have links to other sites, but I do not want the person who comes to my site, to leave and go somewhere else. Therefore with wrappers, you hold their interest. Wrappers are similar to Weblinks, it just the new website they are navigating too, is incased in your website.

Let's play with the top menu for this tutorial. We are going to change all the top menu items to wrappers.

How you do this, go to the toolbar Menu/Top Menu.

The top menu is the bar across the top of your website, which says About Joomla, Features, News and community.

Figure 91: Top Menu

Let's change this to all wrappers. Since there are already menu items, you can either put a checkmark on each one and click the trash icon or click the menu item name or open up each one and change type within the detail screen.

Figure 92: Menu Item Detail Screen

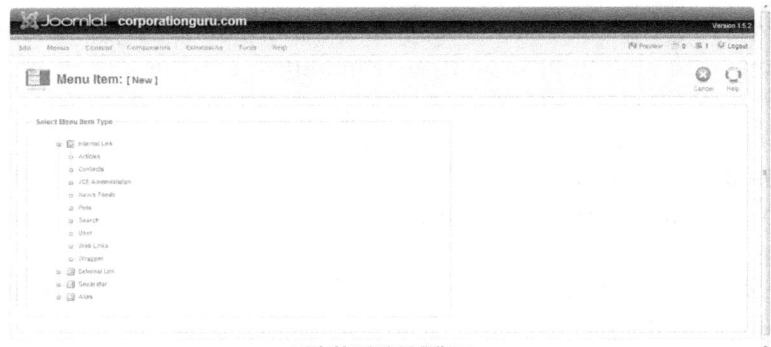

For my website, I am just going to click Change Type and change the menu item to wrapper.

A wrapper is different than a Weblink, in that the link box you need to leave alone.

The wrapper website goes on the right hand side under link.

Figure 93: Wrapper

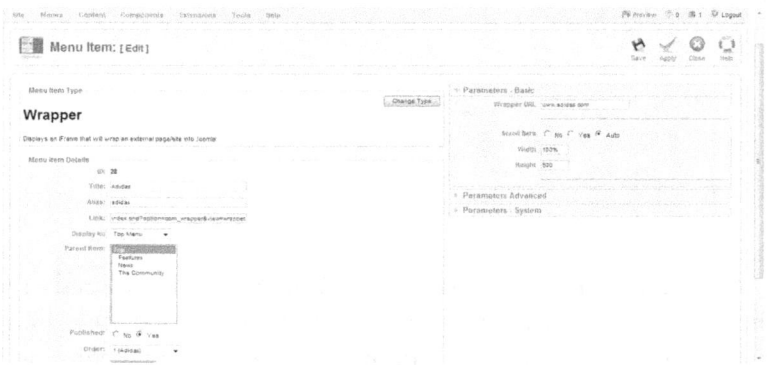

In the example, this wrapper is the Adidas website; notice the link on the right hand side where the website address goes. Once you add your first wrapper and refresh your website.

If you click your you new menu item on the top menu the website which is a wrapper will open in the middle of your screen.

Figure 94: Website Wrapper

Go ahead and change all your top menu links to wrappers, if you wish.

Figure 95: Website with top menu changed

Updating the Logo

We need to change the logo from Joomla to your website name. Each template has a different logo name. Typically we would have to find it.

Since we are using the default template of rhuk_milkway, we need to find the logo within the template file.

To change logo you will need a program which can create .png or .jpg files. If you have Photoshop or another program the logo size is 1 inch (width) by .21 inch (height) using a transparent background.

I assume that most people buying this book, may not have access to a program which creates .png or .jpg; I have enclosed a coupon at the back of the book, for you to have a professional logo created for you. All you have to do is provide proof of purchase of this book, and a Graphic Design artist will work with you to create the logo you need for your site.

I recommend you begin this process right away, once you read this because a logo takes on average a few days of back and forth to meet your desired look and specifications.

If you have a program, go ahead and create your logo. For the rhuk_milkway template you will need to name it mw_joomla_logo.png I recommend keeping the same name when you save your file, then you don't have to go into the actual template and change the code.

The logo file is located within the Cpanel/File Manager. Go back to the Cpanel chapter if you don't remember how to access

it. Once the File Manager opens go to the Template folder, then
double click and go to the rhuk_milkway folder/images.

Figure 96: Image Folder

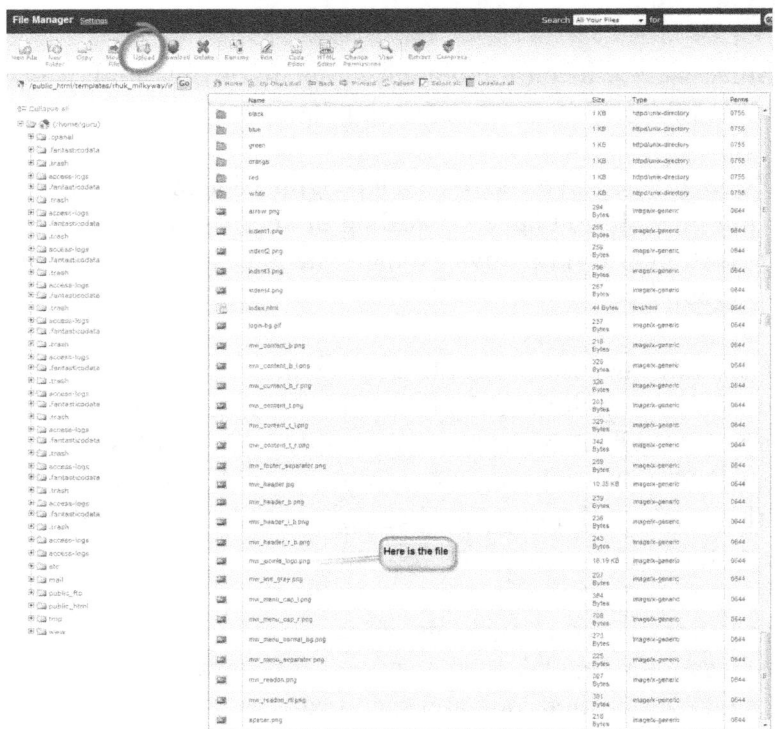

Do you see the mw_joomla_logo.png in the screen shot. At
the top of the screen, there is a circle around the upload icon on
the screen shot.

Click the upload button to browse and find your file.

Then click upload. When it asks to replace file, click YES. The image will now upload.

Figure 97: Upload

Figure 98: Replace File

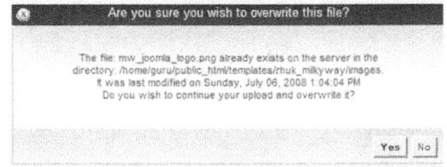

Figure 99: Upload Complete

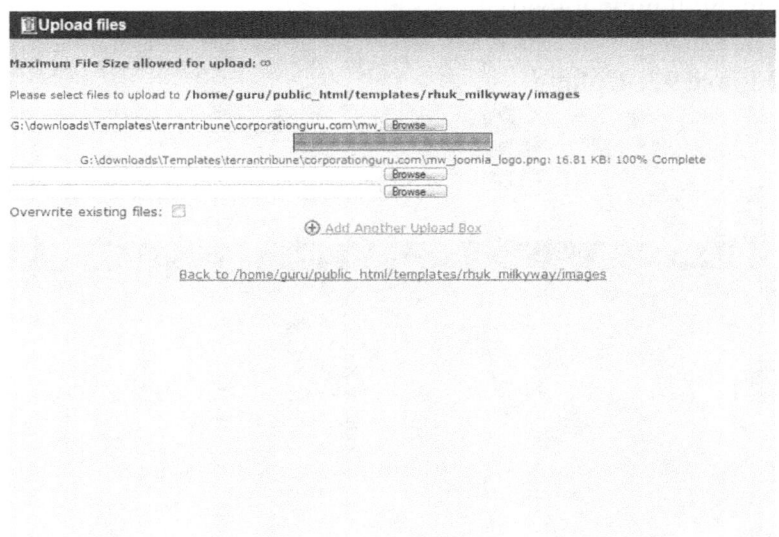

Go ahead and refresh your website your new logo should be there.

Figure 100: Website with new Logo

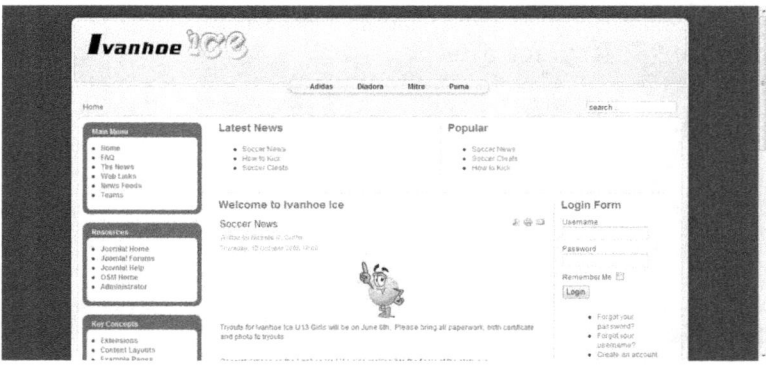

Media Manager

Before we go too much farther, you need to learn about the Media Manager and adding images to your site. The Media Manager and adding images to your site. The Media Manager is located under Site/Media.

Figure 101: Media Manager

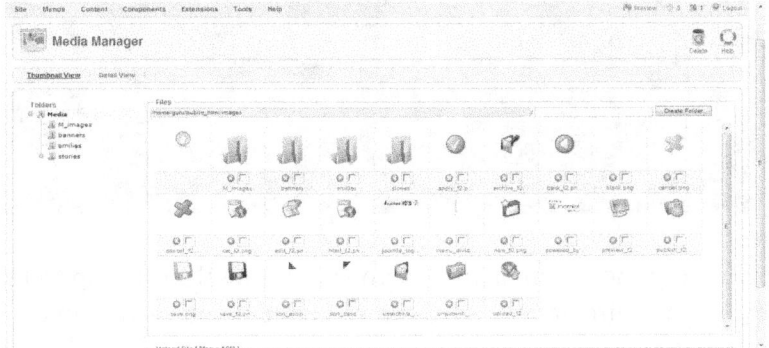

If you click the Banners folder on the left hand side, this is where the Banner images are stored. The banners will be discussed in the next section. But if you look at your website, the Joomla Shop is a banner at the bottom of your site.

Figure 102: Banner Media Manager

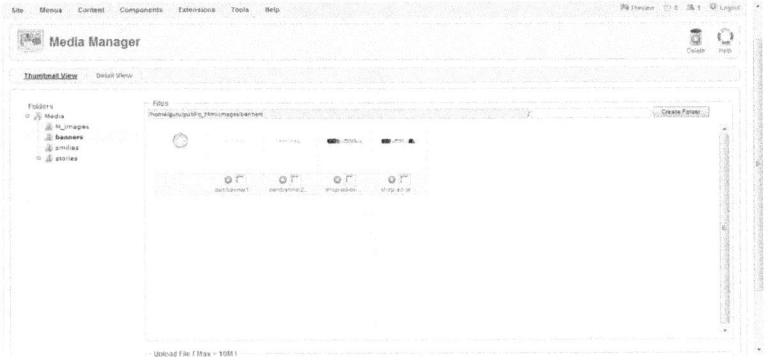

If you click on the image, it will enlarge it.

Figure 103: Banner Image enlarge

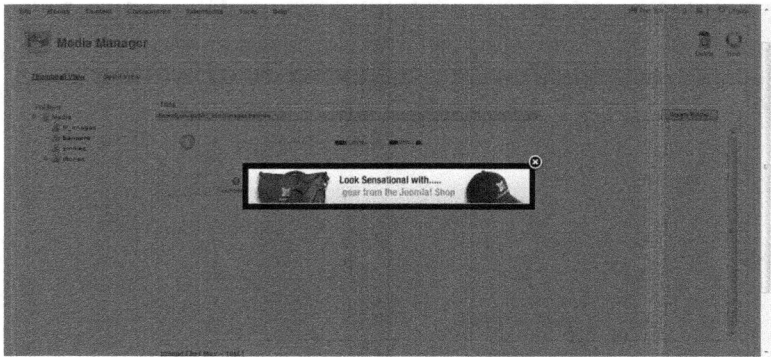

Clicking the green arrow on your screen will bring up to the next higher directory or you can navigate using the menu on the left hand side.

Let's click on Stories and look and see what images are in there. Under Stories is where the images you use in Articles are stored. You can delete any of the default icons or keep them. It is up to you.

Figure 104: Media Manager/Stories

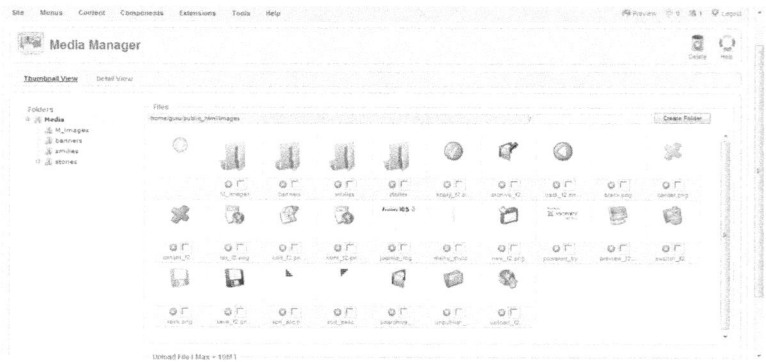

Media Manager is important, because if you are going to use graphics on your website, you will want to load them through here. Do you see the browse button at the bottom of the media manager screen? This is where you upload.

To upload an image from your computer, click Browse and navigate to the folder where your image is stored. Press open and then click Start Upload. The file will upload and tell you when complete; you will also see an image with the other images. I uploaded a soccer ball in this example.

Figure 105: Media Manager Upload

Banner Manager

There is a neat feature in Joomla called Banners. Banners allow you to have advertising on your site, if you wish. Banners are changed under components/Banners and displayed through the Module Manager. If you refresh your website, you will see two Banners on your site.

Figure 106: Website Banners

The first on the right tool bar labeled Advertisement and at the bottom of the website showing a Joomla Store banner.

Let's update the Banner Categories first. Banners is located under component//Banners.

Figure 107: Banner Manager

There are a number of default Banners. Let's modify some of the banners for your site.

Ultimately you will need to be able to create .jpg's or .png's in order to add images to your Banner ads.

But, we will walk you through the process, if you are not ready to mess with Banners, then you can go to the Module Manager (Extensions/Module Manager) and disable Banners.

First let's update categories for one of the banners. I am going to change the first category to Soccer and change the last category to Promo only.

Figure 108: Banner Categories

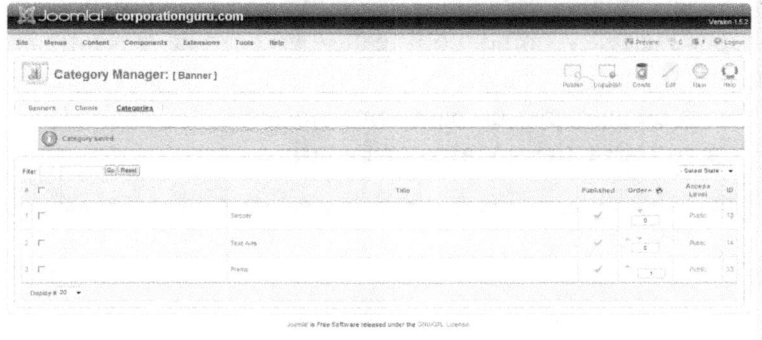

Let's click on the clients tab within the Category Manager. The link is just below the Category Manager name. There is only one client, let's change it to something that fits your site.

Figure 109: Banner Client Manager

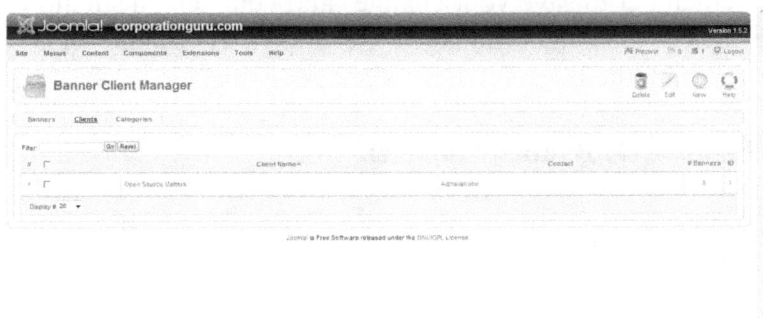

Click on the Client Name and change the name to something appropriate for your site. I am changing mine to "Soccer Advertising".

If you decide to sell space on your site, then you can set this up as actual client names, track hits and then charge them for space usage. Another cool feature you can have rotating banners, therefore you can have different clients and have different banners pop up based on settings.

Figure 110: Client Manager Detail

Remember to save your changes and your screen should be back at the Client Manager. Let's click the Banner link underneath the Banner Client Manager name.

Figure 111: Banner Manager

Click on the first Banner name in this case it is Joomla Promo
Shop.

Figure 112: Banner Detail

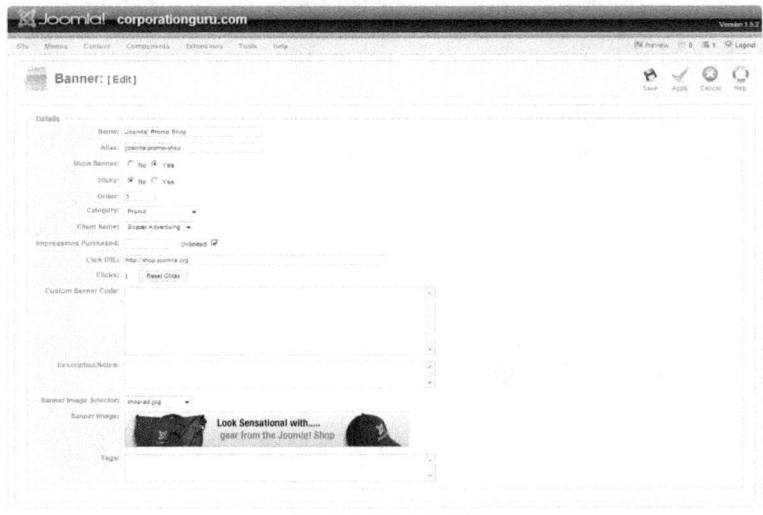

Since I do not have any clients for this site, I am going to use
the Banner placement to show the soccer characters. This will
show you generally what you need to do for adding a banner
campaign.

Banner campaigns' can be profitable; if you have a high track
site those pennies add up. Look at where Google makes all their
money. It is from the click through.

Fields:

• Title: Name of Banner
• Alias: Name of Banner with no spaces
• Show Banner: Yes or No
• Sticky: Yes or No (Means it is a static banner and does
not change)

• Order: position of banner compared to other banners.

• Category: The category showed in the Banner module is selected in the module detail for Banner. In this instance, I have it set as Promo.

• Impressions Purchased: How many times do you want the banner to appear before the end of the campaign.

• Click URL: If the banner is clicked what site does it navigate to.

• Custom Code: You can add html or Java Script code to have the banner do additional functionality.

• Banner Image: Select image which is stored in Site/Media Manager/Banner

• Tags: Keyword which are tagged by the search engines.

Figure 113: Banner Detail Page

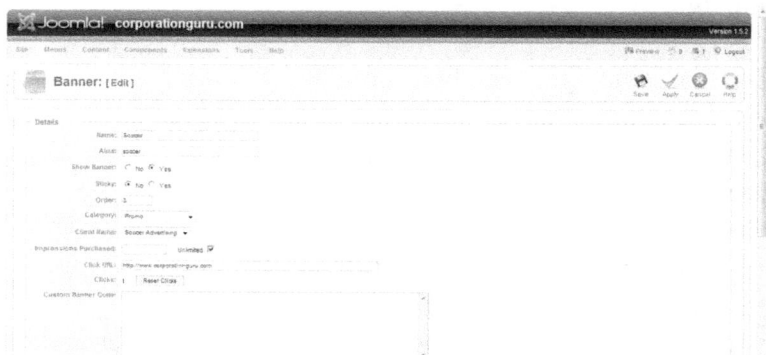

If you go to Extensions/Module Manager and open the Banner Module, you will see the detail fields which state how images from the Banner modules are transitioned.

Figure 114: Banner Module

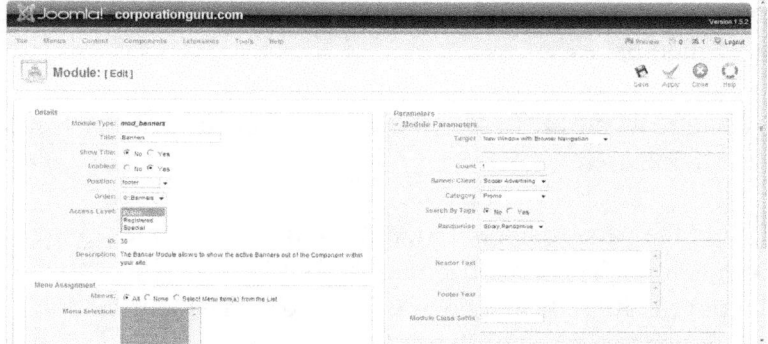

The right hand columns control how banners are displayed.

• Target: Do you want the banner when clicked to navigate to the new website or open a new session. When clicking a banner, you do not have the option of a wrapper. Therefore I recommend have the navigation open a new window. Then your website is still visible on the other session. If selecting new window, I recommend no browser navigation. Therefore they have a higher probability of exiting that session and going back to your site.

• Banner Client: Leave as Select Client if this banner does not run just a specific client.

• Category: Select what category the banner will be pulled from.

• Randomize: Sticky, Randomize or Stick, Ordering this is taken from the Banner where the order and stickiness were selected.

The bottom of the left hand column is selection of what pages the banner is to show up on. You can select all or select individual pages.

Change whatever fields you need to change to fit your website and click SAVE.

Now the Advertisement module is also tied to the Banner Component. The advertisement module looks similar to the Banner module. If you open up the Advertisement module you noticed it uses a different Category. But, also notice that the default Joomla site add code into the footer text on the right hand side, this adds a link to a website with the text "Ads by Joomla". You can either delete this code or change it to navigate where you desire.

Figure 115: Advertisement Module

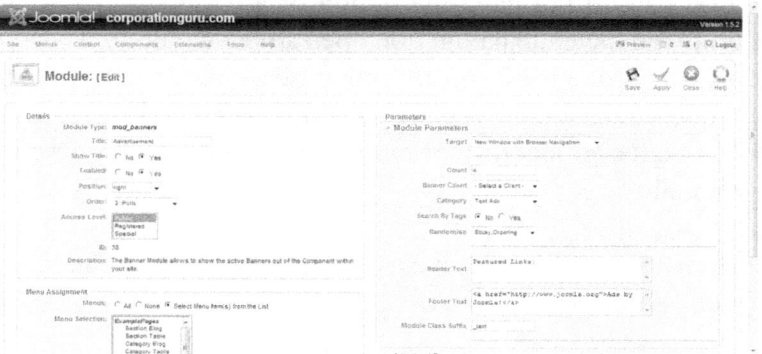

But for the website we are building, I am doing to disable this module. Because in a few chapters we are going to begin adding modules from components we will download from www.joomla.com. If you need then alter it as you see fit.

While we are in the Module Manager, I am also going to turn off the Resources module, Extensions module and Example Pages.

I am also going to move the Login Form to the Left column underneath the main module. Go ahead and re-arrange your page, to how you would like to see it. Don't worry about spaces, we are going to be adding more modules to the website.

The demonstration website now looks like this.

Figure 116: Ivanhoe Ice Website

Search

The search component in Joomla is a handy tool. If turned on, then when someone searches your website, it records searches. Then you can modify your site to contain the items your customers would like to see on your site.

To turn this feature on, just go the search component under Component/Search.

Figure 117: Search

Once you change the parameter to Yes, go to your website and search for content. Then come back to the Search component and you will see that it recorded the search.

Figure 118: Search Recording

User Manager

To access the User manager go to Site/user Manager.

Figure 119: User Manager

Let's look at the detail screen of your user. Click the User name and we will look at the details.

Figure 120: User Manager Detail

We briefly looked at the User Manager when we installed the JCE Component. But now we are going to add a user to Joomla. We are not going to add it from the back end, we are going to pretend we are a new user and add it from the login module on your website. Let's go to your website and Create an Account underneath the Login module.

Figure 121: User Login

The fields are very simple to register. You have to use a different email, then the one you are using for administration. Your hosting company allows you to setup additional email addresses. Go back to the email chapter in order to create a second email address to test your login module.

Figure 122: Registration

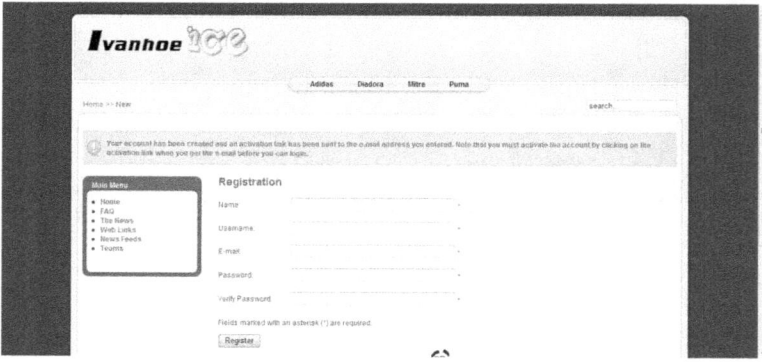

Let's fill this out. Click Register. If registration is successful the following message appears to your customers.

Now go back to your User Manager and refresh. Your new customer has just registered.

Figure 123: User Manager with new registration

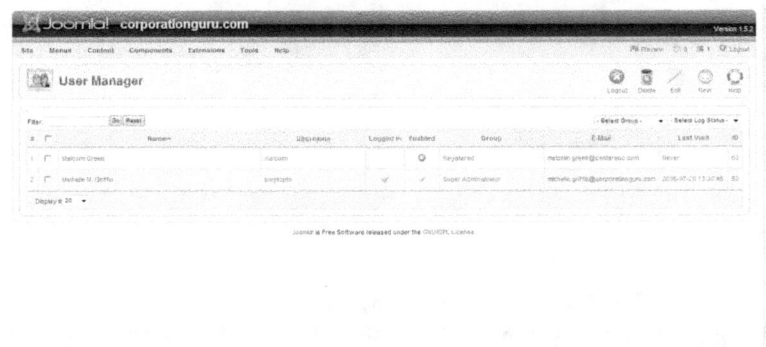

Now check your administration email. There will be an email stating a new user registered.

Figure 124: Email notification of user registration

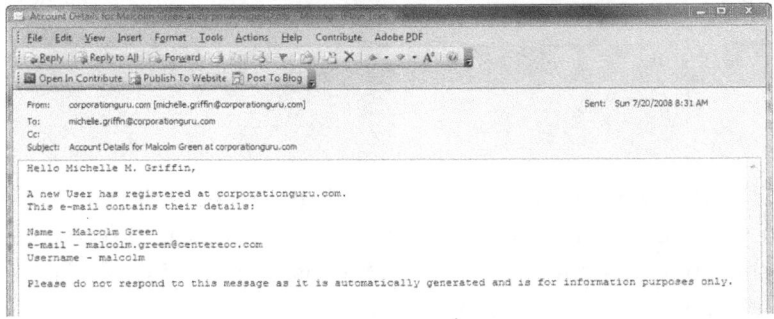

Now, check the email for the user there is a activation link. Click the activation link to activate the account.

Figure 125: Email Notification to New User

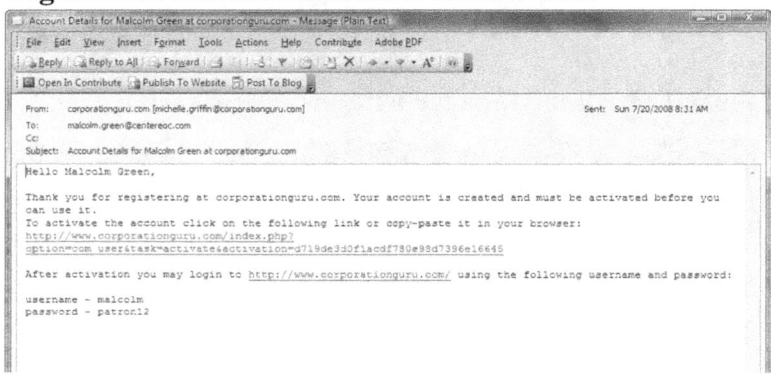

Figure 126: New User Activation

The Activation complete page appears for the new user. Now do you see why I put the Soccer icons in the Banner position, rather than a client add, because this banner is set to show up on every page within the footer.

By using the icon, I made the registration appear friendly. Let's refresh the Joomla dashboard. The user is now enabled.

Figure 127: User Manager Enabled

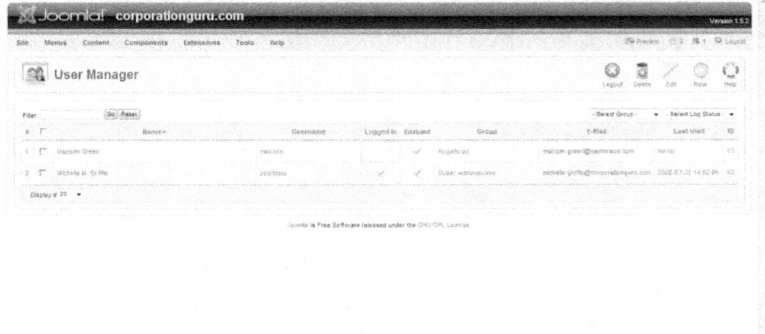

Figure 128: User authorization levels

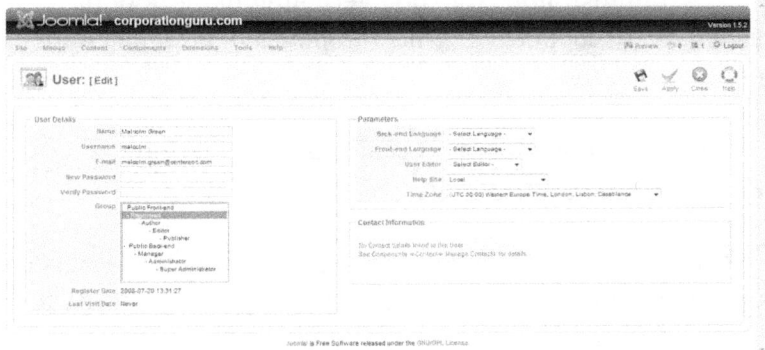

There are different Group levels within User management
- Registered: User can access the website and view registered only modules and content.

- Author: Can submit content to the website, typically through the Submit content menu item. Even though content is submitted it is not posted until a high level group approves the submission.

•   Editor: The user can post and edit any content on the site. But cannot approve the content for publishing.

•   Publisher: This user can post and edit as well as approve posting for content submitted by other users.

Back End Permissions:
•   Manager: Similar to Publisher but able to access the Joomla Dashboard to create content. All modules and features in the back end are disabled except for what they are authorize to modify.

•   Administrator: Can do everything in the Joomla Dashboard, except change Site Templates or edit the Global Configuration file.

•   Site Administrator: Has all rights to the Joomla Dashboard.

We are going to leave this user you just created as Registered. But if you notice on the right hand column, it allows you to select User Editor.

This feature can be changed individually for all users or can be changed globally in the Global Configuration file. In order to change it in the Global Configuration file, you will need to go back to the Global configuration chapter and reset the permissions for the configuration.php file.

Then go to Site/Global Configuration and change the Default

WYSIWYG editor to the JCE module or Tiny if that is what you are using. I am going to change it to the JCE module.

Figure 129: Default WYSIWYG Editor:

If you decide to set the Default WYSIWYG Editor then ensure you go back and change the default to 644 in the Cpanel. Once you change this all future users are given the default editor.

All you will need to do is grant access to their groups within the User Module.

Upgrading

Every few months, it is a good idea to go back into your Cpanel/ Fantastico to verify the version of Joomla which is available.

Figure 130: Fantastico upgrade

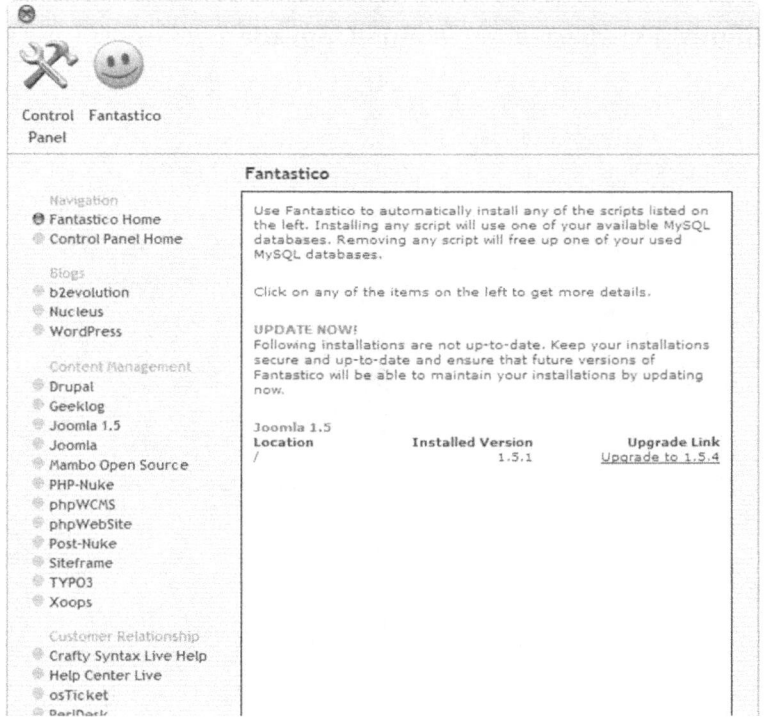

As you can see there is a stable upgrade to Joomla 1.5.4. Let's click the upgrade to 1.5.4.

Realize when you upgrade, it means you may have to reinstall some components and modules for your site.

Any site templates you installed will also be lost and it will revert back to the original Joomla site.

Once you have re-designed your site a few times, you won't be initiated by upgrading. It is not something you do all the time, maybe once or twice a year.

Figure 131: Continue Joomla Upgrade

Overview

In the first section of the Joomla! 1.5, we walked through how to create a basic website. You can be as creative as you wish. Now we are going to enhance a new website and create an e-commerce website which sells product.

For this section, I am going to build a website which I need for selling training software to companies and individuals and it is located at www.corporationguru.com.

The first thing I am going to do is now re-configure my site with a new template. In order to create a more personalized site. I spent about 15 minutes, and below is our starting place for the next section of this book. Now if you are implementing the following types of sites, this section will interest you.

•   Sport Website, with player registration and online payment.

•   Not for Profit website with the ability to accept online donations.

•   Membership website, where members can join and pay dues on line

•   Customer catalog website, where customers can purchase your product online (This feature can be used by the Mom and Pop shop or the largest corporation. It tracks your orders and there is EDI functionality in order to send a flat file to your backend system (i.e. SAP or Oracle- we will not be covering in it in this deep of detail but it can be done).

•   Knowledge database where employees can download files and you can track who downloaded what information.

The functionality is endless from this point; it is a matter of playing and trying different extensions and modules to see what works for your site.

Here is a sample of the new site. To build the site to this point, all I did was change the template to a template from Rocket Theme.

Figure 132: CorporationGuru Website

The Rocket Themes also have a number of module positions. Which allows me the flexibility of moving items around in order to create a unique site.

The module positions give you unlimited functionality to create a site that is personalized to your individual or corporation site.

Figure 133: Module Positions

Virtuemart Installing

Now let's add a shopping cart in order to pay for customer purchases.   Go to www.virtuemart.net.

Figure 134: Virtuemart Website

At the top of the website there is a box, stating download Virtuemart stable version. Let's click this button. It brings you to the download page. We want to download the Virtuemart version for Joomla 1.5.

Figure 135: Virtuemart Download

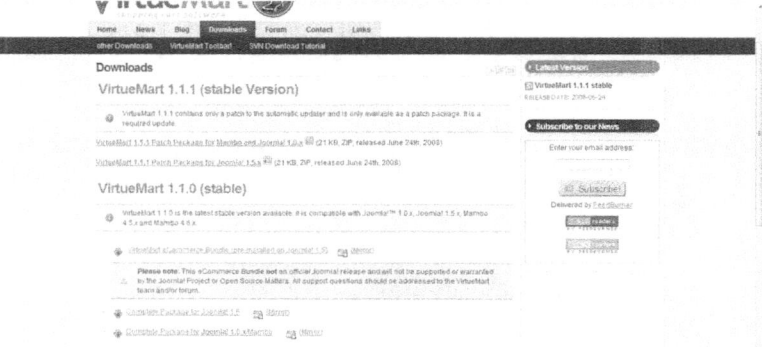

Click on the Virtuemart download for Joomla 1.5. If you look at the download page, there is VirtueMart 1.1.0 (stable) which is the core modules and then there is a patch upgrade also.

Figure 136: Complete Package for Joomla 1.5 download

Click Save and navigate to where you would like to save the file.

Figure 137: Virtuemart Save

Let's download the core module and its components, and then we will add the patch before we begin building our site. Given we are building a new site it is easy to upgrade.

Just remember when you have a full site with your catalog and ordering setup, you must be cautious on upgrading in the future to ensure you don't have to re-enter all your data again.

Given we have already installed Joomla through Fantastico we need to download the Complete package for Joomla 1.5. Go ahead and click on the link and let's download.

I highly recommend you create a separate folder for Virtuemart because there will be a number of files.

Do you see the New Folder icon within the explorer panel which opens when you click save? Click on New folder to save your file.

Once the file is downloaded it is a zip file; which needs to be unzipped. Open Windows Explorer and navigate to your Virtuemart folder. If Windows Explorer is not on your desktop it can be found in your Windows Navigation/All Programs/ Accessories/Windows Explorer.

Figure 138: Windows Explorer Virtuemart Folder

Double click on the Virtuemart file. On the navigation bar, it will stated Extract Files. If your Windows does not have and extractor installed, you can download Winzip or 7 Zip as a trial version to use temporarily or there is freeware zip programs also. Just do a search on your favorite search engine.

Once the Virtuemart file is unzipped your windows explorer looks like this:

Figure 139: Virtuemart Unzipped

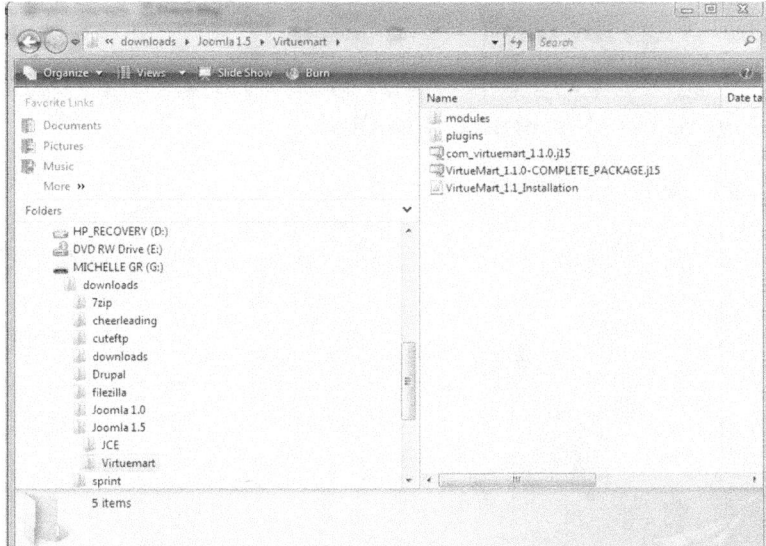

The first one we are going to install is the com_ virtuemart_1.1.0.j15. Let's go into our Joomla Dashboard and install the file.

Go to Extensions/Install, then click browse and find the com file which you have in a folder.

Figure 140: Install Virtuemart

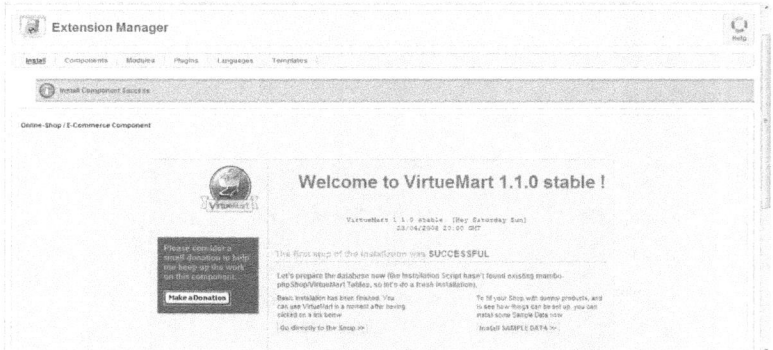

Figure 141: Virtuemart installed

You have two choices to either install the sample data or not. I myself install the sample data then modify it. Mainly because then all fields are filled out and then I know what to change.

Without the sample data, you have to remember to do all the little things, like set up Tax, Country etc….it is easier in my opinion to just go change it.

Figure 142: Virtuemart Store

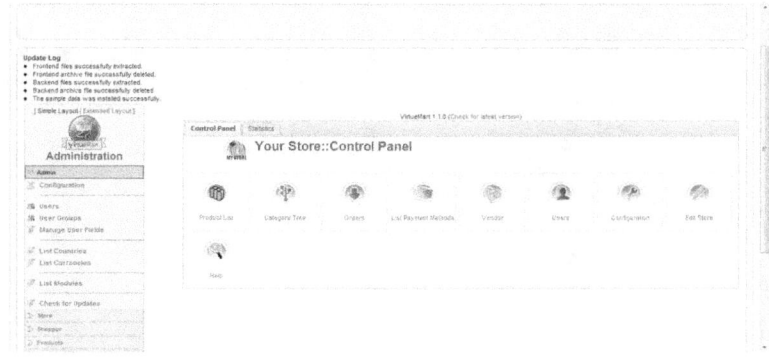

Now, before we do anything we need to upgrade to the patch version. We need to go to the Virtuemart website and download the patch to the latest version.

Figure 143: Virtuemart Download

We need to install the Patch for Joomla 1.5, click on the link.

Figure 144: Virtuemart Patch Download

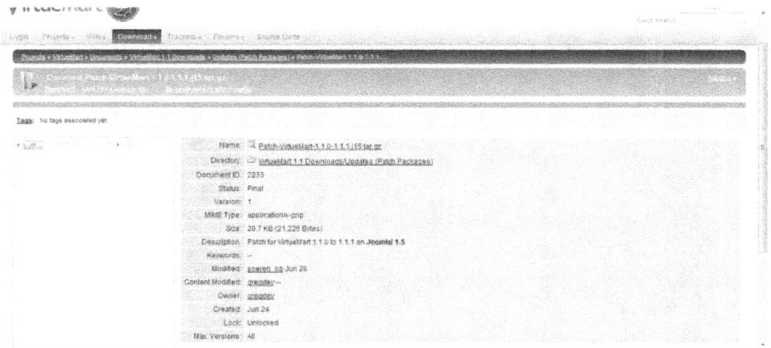

Click on the name of the patch to begin downloading. Save to your Virtuemart directory.

Figure 145: Virtuemart Patch Save

Now go back to your Virtuemart Control Panel. If you are not at the Virtuemart Control panel, it is found under Component/ Virtuemart.   Virtuemart has made it easy to upgrade.   On the left hand side of the Virtuemart control panel there is the admin. There is a little arrow in front of the word Admin, which opens and closes the navigation bar; click on Check for Updates.

Figure 146: Virtuemart Check for Updates

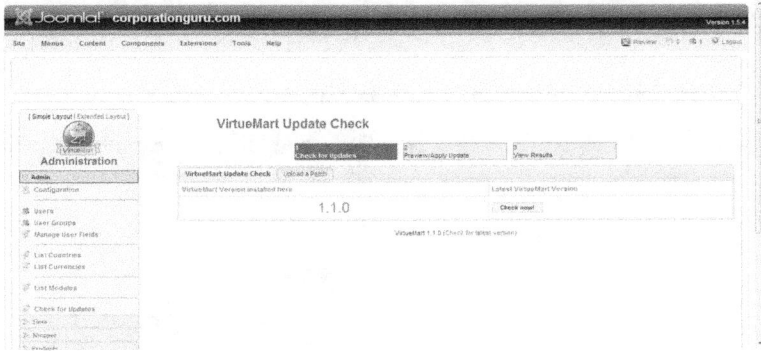

Click the button to check now. This will tell you what updates need to be updated. Sometimes, I receive connection fail when I try it. Therefore, since we already downloaded the patch at the Virtuemart site. We need to click the tab Upload a Patch.

Figure: 147: Upload a Patch.

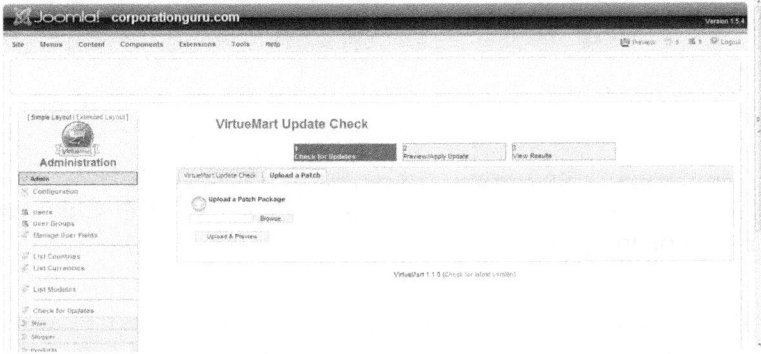

Browse for Patch file, that you just downloaded, then click Upload & Preview.

When you upgrade, realize that some of your content will be lost and you will have to go back and re-enter main Virtuemart screens, for instance Configuration, Store Summary, etc....

It does not typically lose order information, unless it is a major upgrade, just be very careful with upgrading.

Figure 148: Virtuemart Patch Upgrade

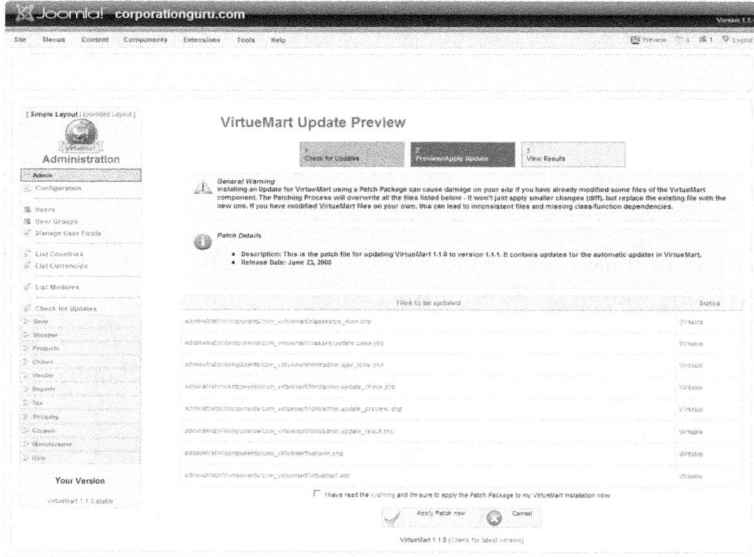

The list of files to be updated, will tell you basically what items you will need to re-update once the install is through.

Once you reviewed the patch then check the box stating "I have read the Warning" and click Apply Patch now.

Figure 149: Virtuemart Patch upgrade Finished

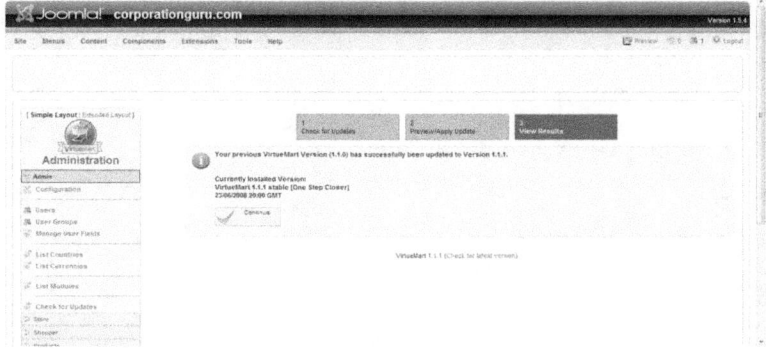

Press Continue and Virtuemart is now installed within your website. But it is not showing to your customers until we customize it.

Virtuemart Configuration

Now let's go to the Virtuemart Control Panel and select Admin/Configuration.

Figure 150: Virtuemart Admin

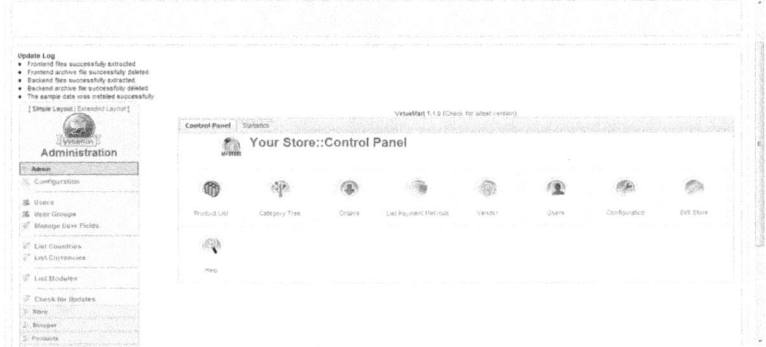

I recommend staying with the defaults, but changing only a few items, because there is quite a few buttons. If you change something in the future, change one item at a time save and see how it functions.

Global Features:

Shop Offline: Check this only if your shop is offline.

Shop Offline Message: You can customize this to a personal store message.

Use only as Catalogue: Check this if you would customers to be able to view your products but not place an order online. Maybe you would like to have them call in their order or fax it in. This disables the cart functionality.

Figure 151: Virtuemart Configuration

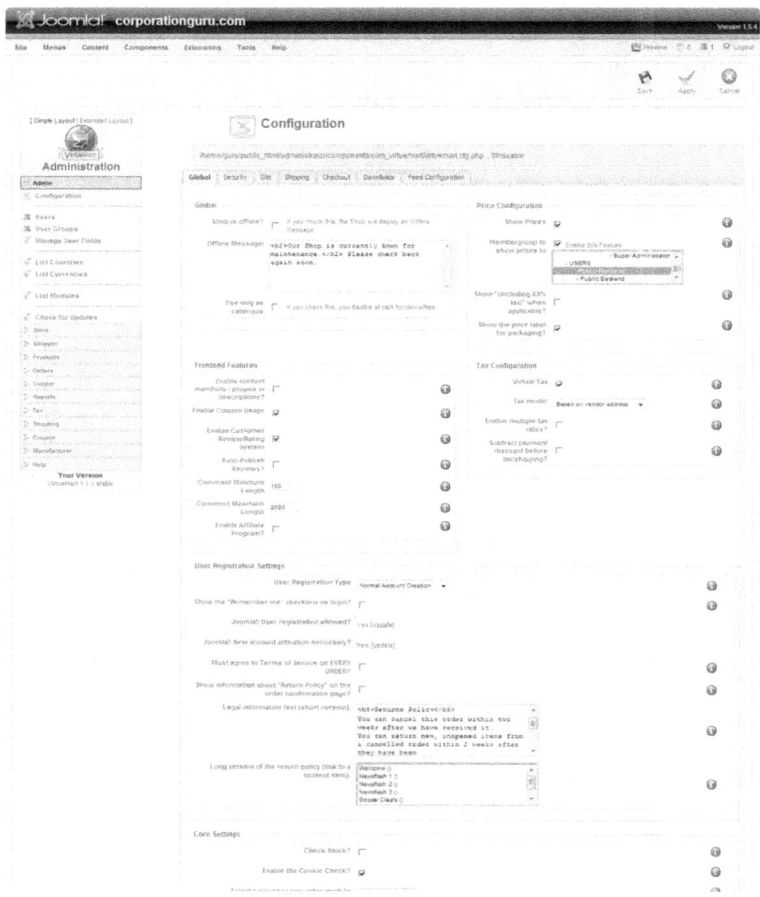

Front End Features:

Enable Content Mambots/Plugin Descriptions: This takes the descriptions from the Plugin versus from Virtuemart.

Coupon Usage: This allows customers to enter discount codes to receive discounts. If you are not offering discounts then Uncheck this box.

Enable Customer Review Rating: This allows customers to rate your product. If you don't require ratings then turn this off.; if you don't know then leave it on for no.

Auto Publish Reviews: Only check this box, if you do not care to review comments on your products. I recommend this stays unchecked. This gives you the control of whether a review is published, which is unfairly negative.

Comment Minimum Length and Maximum Length: How much detail do you want from a customer posting a review.

Affiliate Program: At the writing of this book, this future does not fully work. Please do not check.

Price Configuration

Show Prices: Allows prices to show with your product.

Member group to show prices to the default is "Public Frontend". Public Backend is registered users can only see prices.

Show tax when applicable: Customer will see the tax to be added on.

Show the price label for packaging: Shows customers the pricing per package versus unit.

Show Prices including tax? Customers will see the price with tax included. This I usually check.

Tax Configuration

Virtual Tax: This feature determines if items with zero weight is taxed.

Tax mode: The tax rate is used for calculating taxes for the customer. The tax rate is based on either the Vendor's address or the Customers Address.

Enable multiple tax rates: This you need enabled if you have different taxes for different products.

Discount before tax/shipping: Subtracts the coupon discount prior to calculation of tax. If you are offering discounts or coupons then you want this checked.

User Registration Settings

User Registration Type: There are four different types of User Registration:

- Normal Account Creation: This is a standard registration where the customer must register prior to placing an order.

- Silent Account Creation: This method is a username and password is automatically generated based on the email address. I don't recommend this, because customers are constantly forgetting their passwords, if they do not change it to something they remember.

- Optional Account Creation: A customer can optionally create an account.

- No Account Creation: Checkout occurs within an account.

Show the "Remember me" checkbox on login? This feature sets a cookie on the customers' computer, in order for them to not have to login each time. This is a security threat and not recommended to be turned on.

Agree to Terms of Service on EVERY ORDER: Check this only if every time a customer purchases you want them to agree to your terms of service. This is personal, and based on the type of website you are running. I personally will not have it turned on.

Show information about "Return Policy" on the order confirmation page? If you are selling a product, by law you must have a return policy. This should be checked.

Legal information text (short version): This is your Return policy, read through the standard and make changes which fit your product you are selling.

Long version of the return policy (link to a content item): This is the actual return policy with all the caveats. This is an article written in the article manager, and selected here to be published.

Core Settings

Check Stock: Verifies there is stock available for this item.

Show Products that are out of Stock? Allows you to show Out of Stock product.

Enable the Cookie Check? Allows you to check and see if a customer accepts cookies. I do not set this.

Currency Converter Module: Looks to convert currency, I recommend you leave this as default.

Order-mail format: The setup of your order confirmations either text or html email is sent.

Logging:

I would leave off, logging could create a large file and could deteriorate your server response time.

Figure 152: Virtuemart Global Custom Settings

Let's click on the Security tab and set these parameters. For my site, I am not changing anything on this page.

Figure 153: Virtuemart Security

I recommend leaving this page as the default setting. The only setting you may want to check is the Allow Frontend Administration for non-backend users.

If you have a lot of products to manage, you may want to grant access to users with special privileges' to update the products.

Click on the Site tab now, in order to review these settings.

Site Configuration
PDF - Button : Show or hide the PDF button

Show the "Recommend to a friend" button? Show or hide the link to recommend a friend

Show the "Print View" link? Show or Hide the link for the print view page.

Figure 154: Virtuemart Site

Show Page Navigation at the Top of the Product Listing? Similar to Breadcrumbs in Joomla shows page navigation when down multiple product levels.

Default Product Sort Order: Allows you to select the default sorting of either Product, Price, SKU or Latest Products

Available "Sort-by" fields: The customer can sort their products by Product, Price, SKU or Latest Products.

Show the Number of Products? Shows the number of products in a category; a good feature to have turned on.

"no image" image: Image shown when there is no product image.

This is located in /components/com_virtuemart/themes/ default/images/noimage.gif if you wish to replace the generic image.

Show footer "powered by...": This displays a VirtueMart Footer image.

Layout

Global Shop Theme: You can add custom themes for your Virtuemart Shop.

Default number of products in a row: The number of products per row. I recommend setting this after you site is setup and looking at the best layout.

Category Template: Defines the category template for displaying products. Again, I would wait until your site is setup before changing this, in order to see what looks best.

FLYPAGE: This displays the page which appears when displaying your product. I would wait to modify this until you site is setup.

Dynamic Thumbnail Resizing? This dynamically resizes the thumbnail images for you, this creates higher quality images.

Note: you must have PHP's GD2 enabled on your server.

You can check if you have GD2 support by going to your Joomla Dashboard and navigating to

Help/ System Info, click on the tab for "PHP Info" and scroll down until you see gd.

Thumbnail Image Width and Height : Width and Height of Thumbnail image. Leave as default.

Figure 155: Virtuemart Site

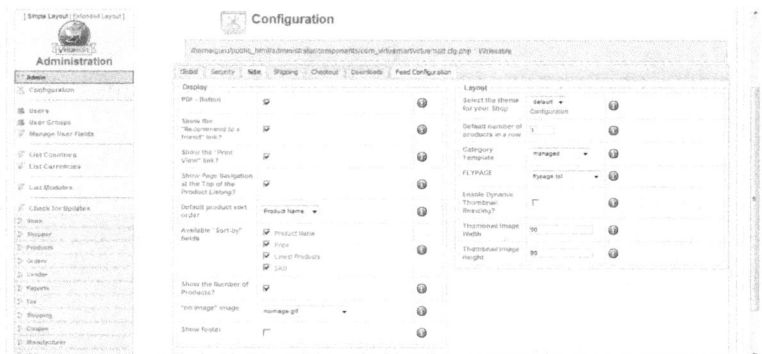

The next tab is Shipping, let's look at the parameters for this screen.

Figure 156: Virtuemart Shipping Config

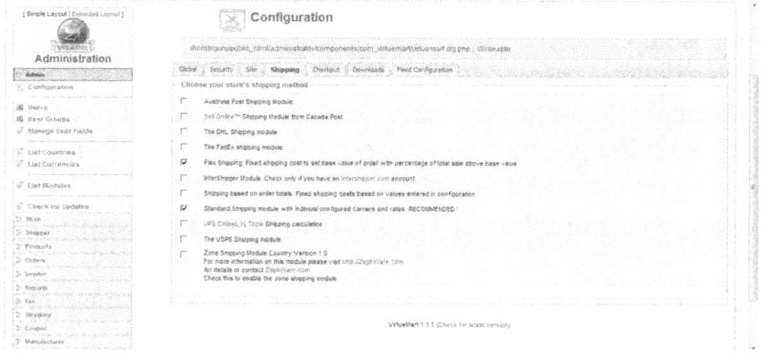

The shipping module is very flexible and if you have DHL, FEDEX or UPS accounts you configure them to access your account for rates and billing.

You will need to go to the Virtuemart site for configuration of these accounts.

If you will not be charging shipping then you need to disable this module as well as in the Checkout process change the shipping verification.

At this time, I will leave everything default for the demonstration site. Let's click the next tab, which is Checkout.

Figure 157: Virtuemart Checkout Config

I recommend leaving this as a default, unless you do not offer shipping then you would uncheck the second box.

The Checkout Bar tells customers what stage of the ordering process they are in, it is very handy for customers.

The stages are numbered, and you can change the order of the stages by changing the number assigned to the stage.

Now let's proceed to the Download configuration page.

This page is only for those who sell downloaded products. Since this site will have downloads. I am going to check this box.

Figure 158: Virtuemart Download Config

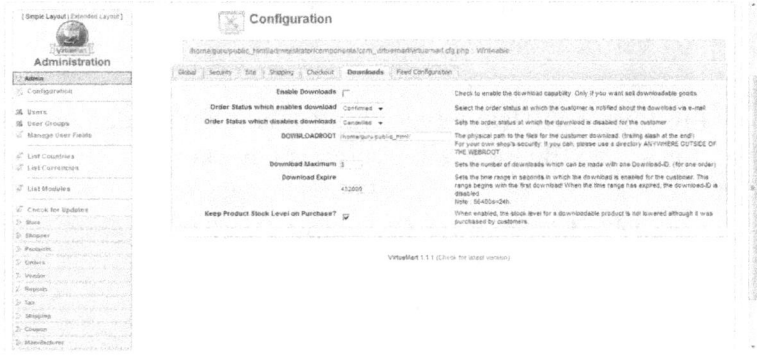

The last configuration file is Feeds. This is found on the last tab.

Figure 159: Virtuemart Feeds Config

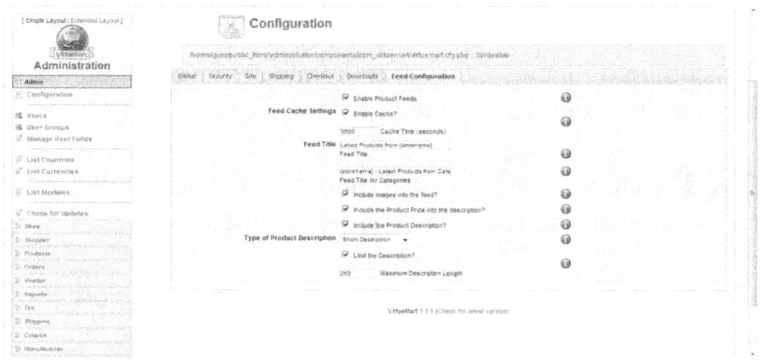

This feature is pretty cool, your customers upon registration can subscribe to a feed, which would send them product updates automatically. For now, let's just leave the default in place. That is it for the configuration file. Let's set up the store information now.

Virtuemart Store

Let's update the store information. The store information is located on the left navigation under Store.

Figure 160: Store Navigation

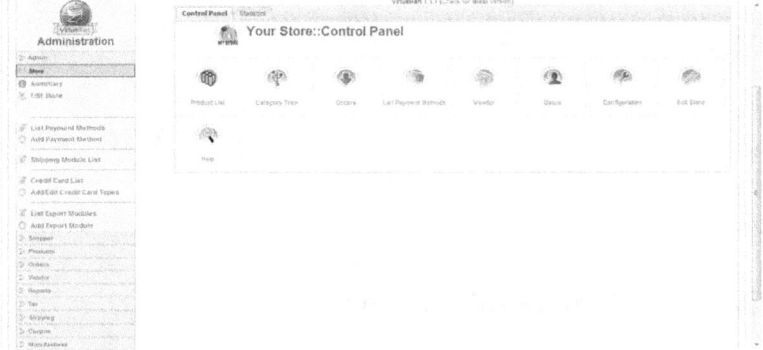

Let's click on Edit Store

Go ahead and change the detail information in the Store to your information.

Then click on the image field and browse for your logo from your website, click save.

Your Store information is shown, if you still need to finish editing then re-click on the Edit Store link.

Don't forget to scroll to the bottom of the Edit store screen to update the description of your company.

One last thing to do, under Currency Display Style in the Thousand separator field you need to enter a comma.

Figure 161: Store Summary

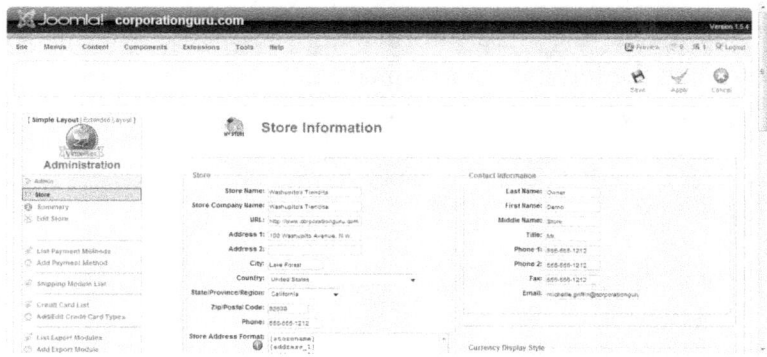

Figure 162: Store Information

Virtuemart Payment Methods

Payment methods are important to configure. If you are a corporation dealing with other corporations, you may need to take Purchase Orders. If you are a company which sells products to customers you may need to take credit cards. But, if you don't have your own credit card processor then you may need to use PayPal.

Figure 163: Virtuemart Control Panel

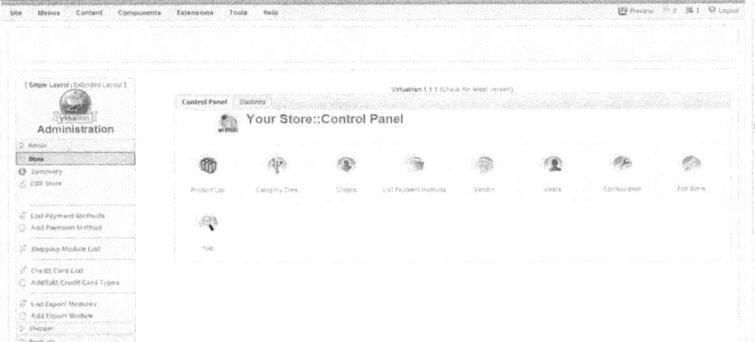

Once the Virtuemart Control Panel opens, on the left hand side under STORE, click on Payment Methods.

As a default the Credit Card, Epay, PayPal, Verisign, Purchase Order and Cash on Delivery are published. For the CorporationGuru website, I will be using only PayPal or Purchase order for right now, therefore I am going to unpublish the other options.

Go ahead and Publish or unpublish what you need for your site.

For this example I will show you how to configure PayPal. To begin, let's open the Virtuemart Control Panel; when in the Joomla Control Panel/Component/Virtuemart.

Figure 164: Payment Methods

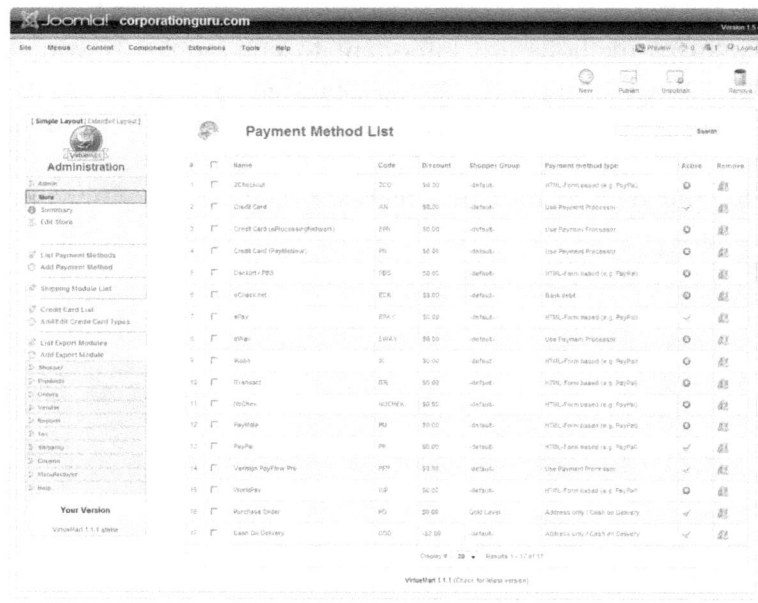

Let's click on Purchase Order and update this first.

Figure 165: Purchase Order Detail

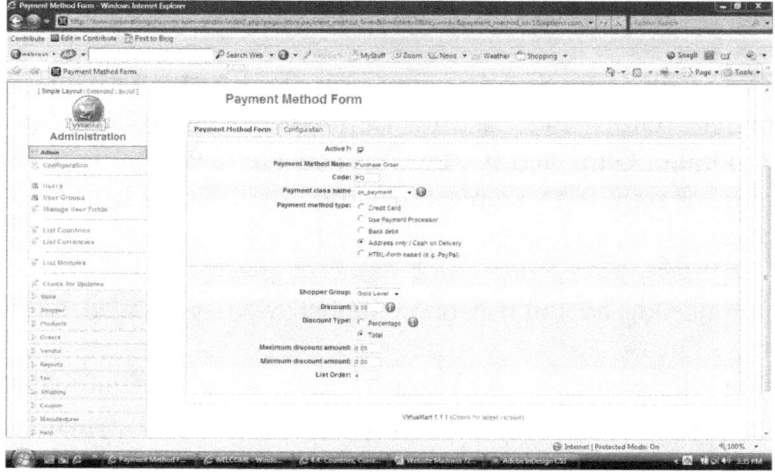

Click the 2nd tab under Configuration and add a little blurbage about this payment method.

Figure 166: Purchase Order Configuration

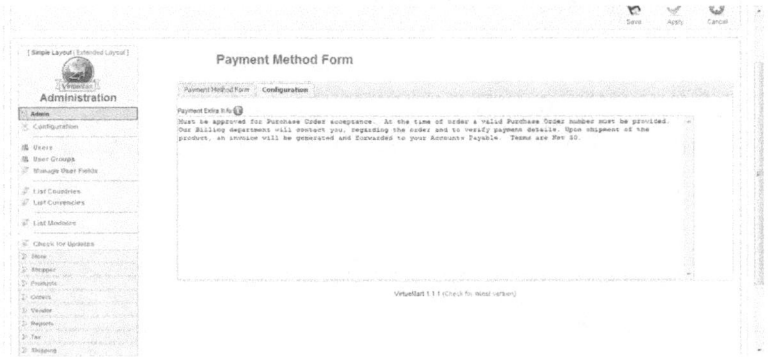

Now, let's configure PayPal. Click on the PayPal link and on the detail page go to Configuration.

Change PayPal Payment email to your email used to access your PayPal account, click save.

Now go back into the Paypal Payment screen and click on configuration again.

Figure 167: PayPal Configuration

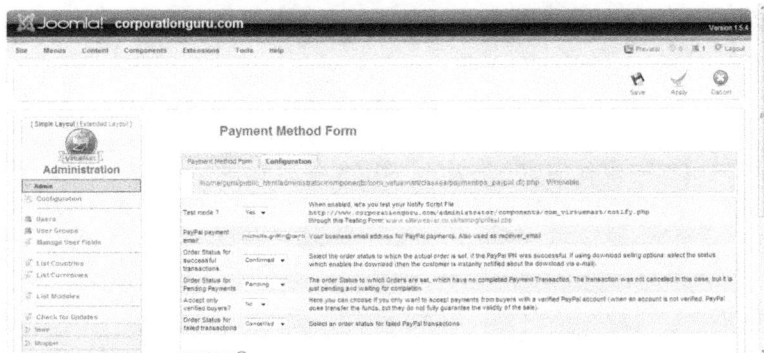

The test mode website for Paypal is down at the time of this writing. You need to change Test Mode to NO.

Figure 168: Paypal Test Mode

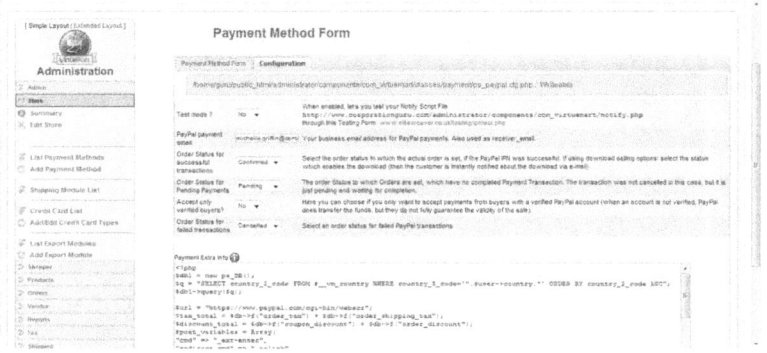

Virtuemart Modules

Before we enter product, let's install the Virtuemart modules. These modules were part of the zip file, which came in the original download. You can install all of them and use what you want or just install the one's you need. I typically install all of them, and then uninstall the one's I do not use.

Figure 169 Modules

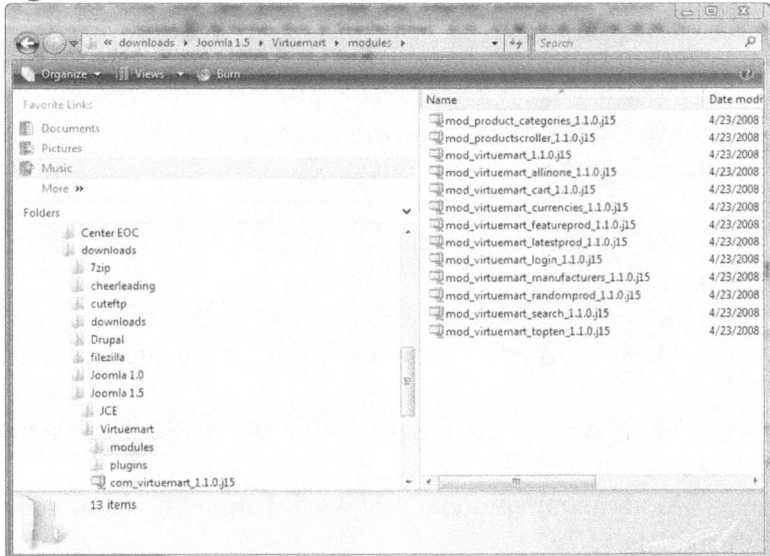

To install, we go to the Joomla Dashboard, click on Extensions/ Install.

Module Descriptions:

• Mod_product_categories – Displays a listing of product categories

• Mod_productscroller – This scrolls your products on the front page of your website.

• Mod_Virtuemart: A combination module with Shopping cart, product search, Administration link, account maintenance link and link to the download page.

• Mod_Virtuemart_allinone: A combination module showing best selling, latest products, featured products and random products.

• Mod_Virtuemart_cart: This is the shopping cart for your customers to make purchases.

• Mod_currencies: Allows customers to select different currencies to pay for their product.

• Mod_Featured Products: Shows a listing of featured products.

• Mod_Latestprod: Shows a listing of the latest products.

• Mod_login: Virtuemart Login replaces the Joomla login.

• Mod_manufacturers: Shows a listing of manufacturers for products.

• Mod_randomprod: Shows a list of random products.

• Mod_virtuemart_search: Allows the customer to search for product.

• Mod_virtuemart_topten: Shows the most popular products.

Browse to the location where your Virtuemart modules are stored and Click on each module to install.

Figure 170: Install

We also need to install Plugins. Within the installer, click browse and go to the Plugin folder. Let's install the plugins.

• Vmproductsnapshots: shows product thumbnails of your product.

• Vmsearch: This is an extended search feature.

Now that everything is installed, let's start activating the modules.

The first one is the Shopping Cart.

Now, you can play around with the module order just by changing the module position in the Module Manager.

Figure 171: Module Manager

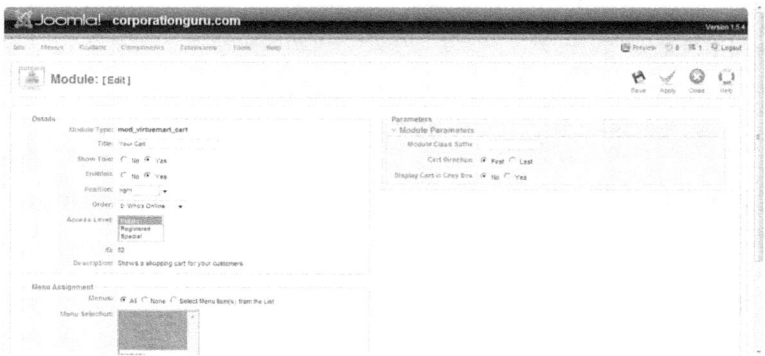

Find the Virtuemart cart module; (Virtuemart Cart) it could be on the first or second page. Click on the module name for the cart and go to the detail page. The first thing we do is change the Cart name to something which fits your site. I usually just rename it "Your Cart".

Figure 172: Virtuemart Cart Detail

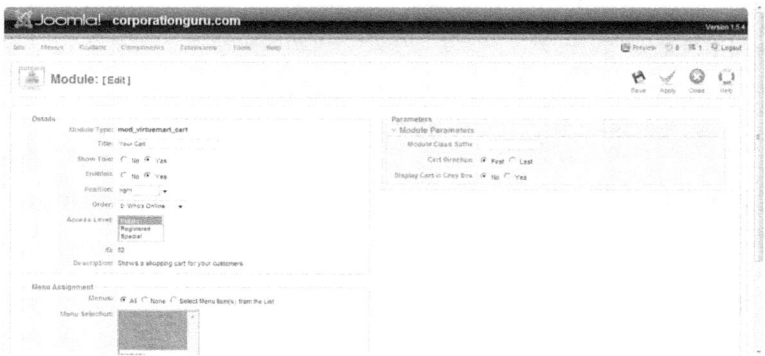

You also have to assign it a position. I have assigned it to the right hand column in the first position.

Under Module parameters on the right hand side, you can set individual parameters for the cart.

• Cart Direction: First or Last –meaning which product is displayed first the first product added to the cart of the last product.

• Display Cart in Grey Box – is just cosmetics, try it and see which way you like best on your website.

Now let's save the cart and refresh the website. Your cart should now appear in the position you put it in. Mine is on the right hand column.

Figure 173: Website Cart

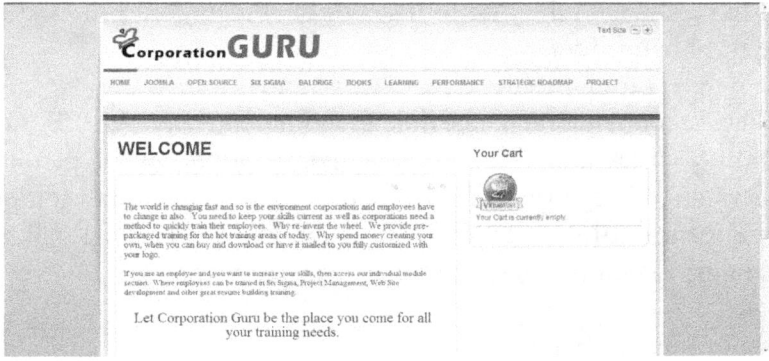

Now let's turn off the Joomla login module and turn on the Virtuemart login module.

Go back to the Module manager and disable the Joomla login. Find the Virtuemart Login module and click the name to go to the details.

Figure 174: Login Module

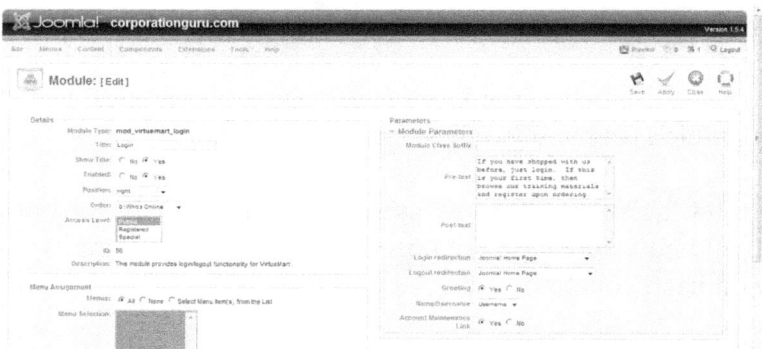

I have changed the title to just Login and entered Pre-Text on the right hand side.

The Account maintenance link, I recommend leaving YES. This is how your customers can review their information and pending orders once logged in. The Account maintenance feature does not appear until the customer is logged in. When done making changes, remember to save and refresh your website.

Now I would like to show Product categories.

Figure 175: Product Categories

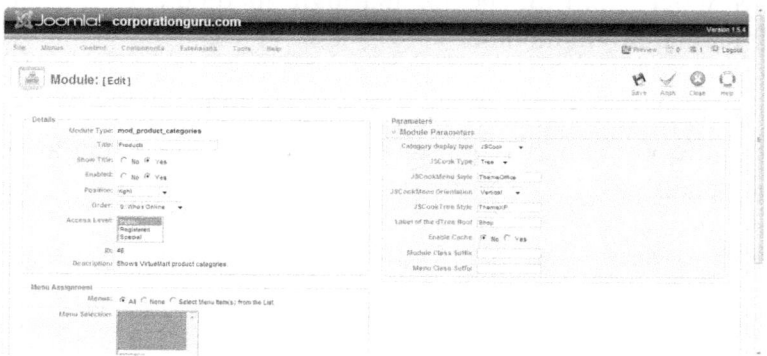

Back on the Module manager listing, let's find the Virtuemart Product Categories modules. Click on the name and let's look at the details.

I changed the Title to Products. I also modified a few of the parameters on the right hand side.

Where it shows JSCook Type: I changed it to Tree from Menu. The Menu option shows the categories with images of the product in front. I personally like the tree. Try them both see which you like.

I also changed the JSCook Menu Orientation to Vertical from Horizontal.

Figure 176: Tree

Remember the website template changed a few chapters ago. Therefore I provide a website view just for your comparison.

Figure 177: Revised Website

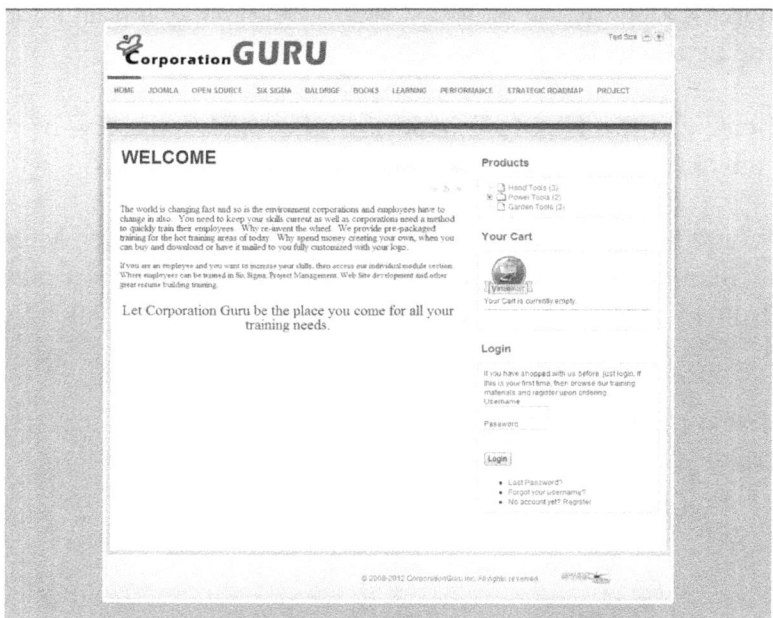

Your website should look similar, with the modules on the right hand side.

Now let's add a few more modules.

Figure 178: All In One

I am going to add a product scroller and the Virtuemart all in one module. I am going to place them in User 4 and User 5 position.

You need to look at your module columns, to know what available positions you have.

First, I changed the title, notice I wrote (Click on the Tabs). The reason for this is this is a tabbed module and I wanted to ensure customers noticed this feature.

Next, drop down the box for Position; you are able to see the available positions. I place this in User 4. I also need to enable this module. One the right hand column under Module Parameters you can modify the settings. I will leave them as default.

Now I am going to add the Product scroller to my site.

Figure 179: Product Scroller

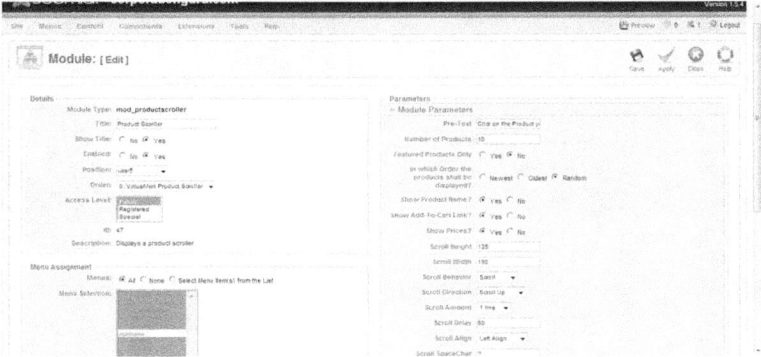

I changed the title to just Product Scroller. I placed this module in User 5 position.

Under Module Parameters, I added pretext letting the customer know to click on the image to view the product. I changed the number of products to 10. But, if you have a lot of products, I would change it even higher unless you have only a few products you want to focus the customer on.

There are many settings for this module. Play with it, until you find the settings that are right for you.

Figure 180: Website Revised

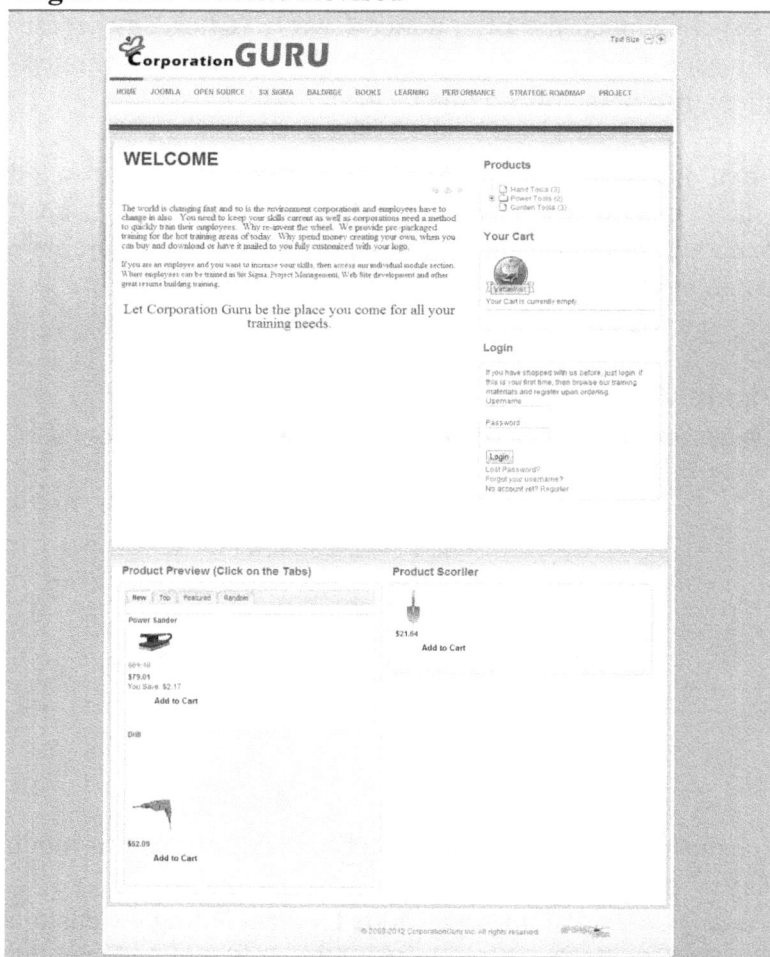

Refresh your website. How does it look?

I noticed on mine, it is off balance, therefore I am going to turn on another module and place it in User 5 to balance the website.

Figure 181: Website with Gaps filled

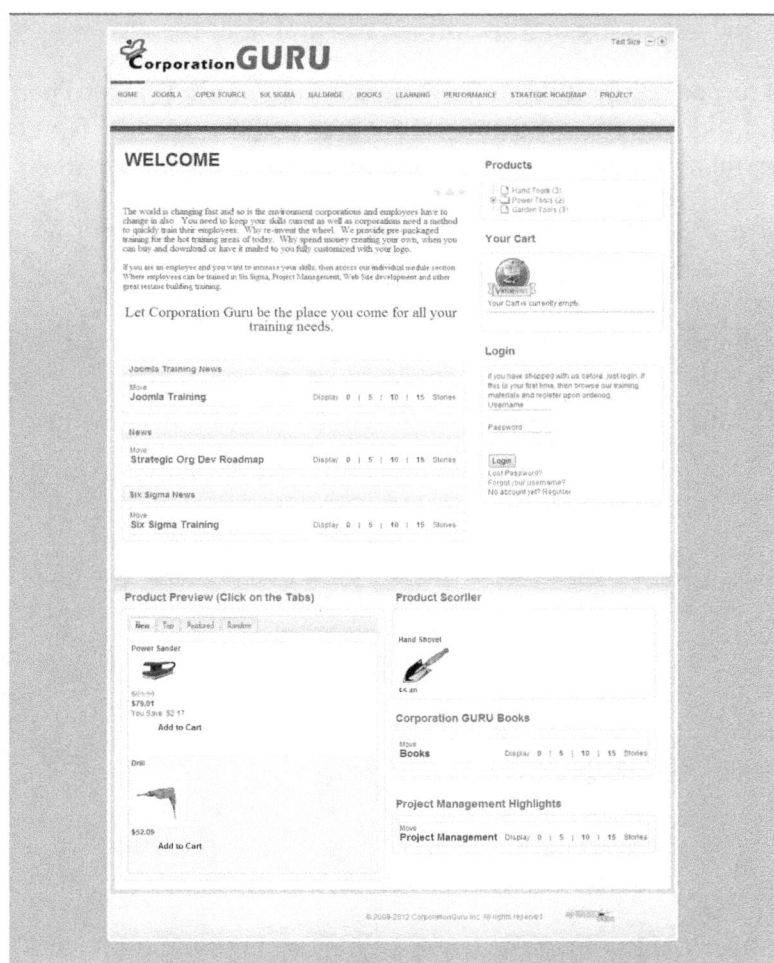

Then I need to add more content to the middle section. Go ahead and modify your website, to give it the appearance you are looking for.

Then let's move on to the next chapter. I am just going to turn on and off some additional modules.

I turned on the Rokmininews which came from Rocket Theme. All I did was copy the module 6 times and renamed it. You can turn on any modules you like based on your website needs.

Virtuemart Tax Rate

Let's set the Tax rates for your store. If you go to the Virtuemart Control Panel on the left hand navigation go to Tax Rate, click on list tax rates.

Figure 182: Tax Rate

Now click on the USA rate and change the default to your home state. You will need to know your tax rate for your state also.

Figure 183: Tax Rate Detail

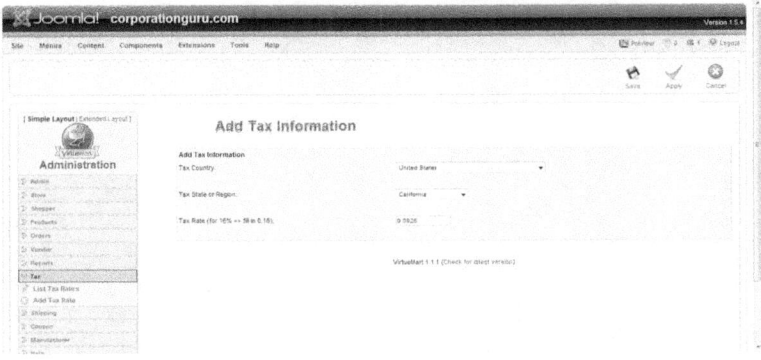

Figure 184: Illinois Tax Rate

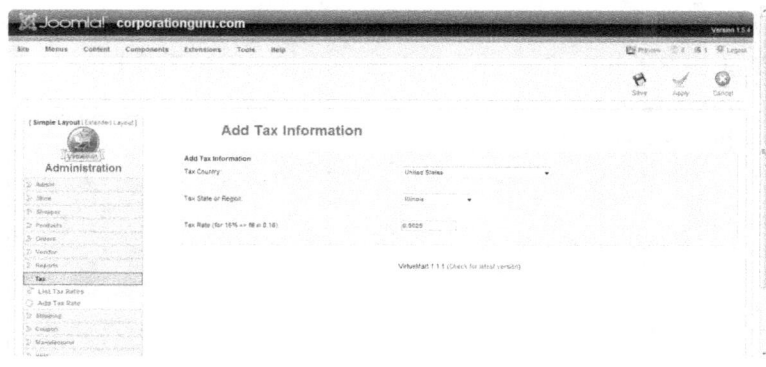

Virtuemart Categories

The product categories are located in the Virtuemart Control panel on the left navigation under Products.

Figure 185: Product Categories

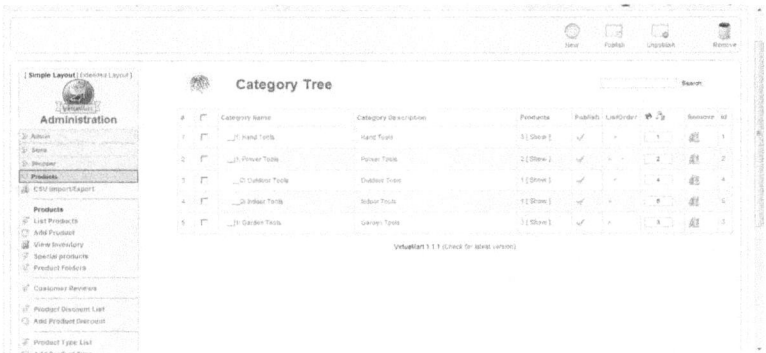

You can either change the categories that are there or delete them and create new ones.

I am just going to change the categories, because then all the fields are filled in. Click on Hand Tools and let's change this one.

At this point I am only changing the name and description.

Once we done, we will come back and adjust the Number of products per row and the Browser page.

Click on the 2nd tab and insert an image.

Figure 186: Product Detail

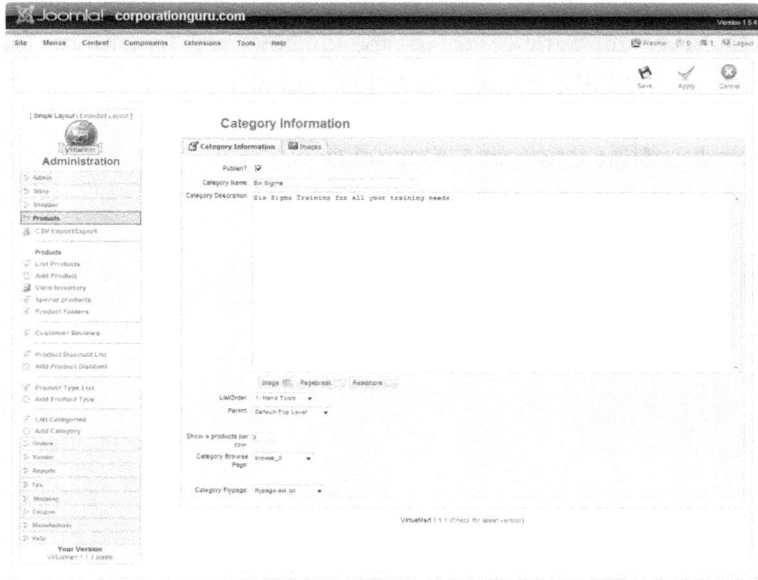

Figure 187: Category Image

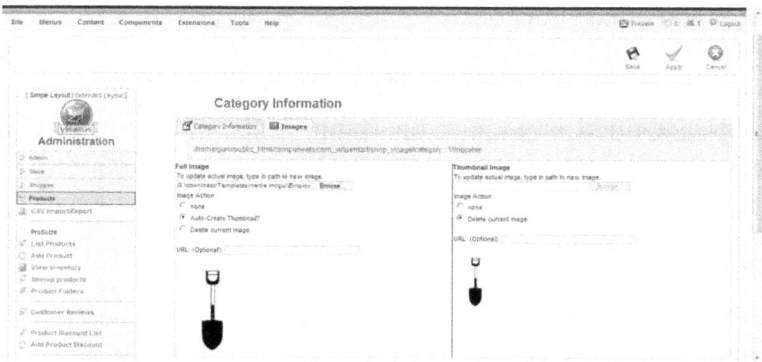

Browse for your image file and check the radio button for Auto-create thumbnail. Then check the radio button for Delete current image under thumbnail and save.

You will exit this screen and go back to the category listing.
Go back in and verify your images appeared.

Figure 188: Image update

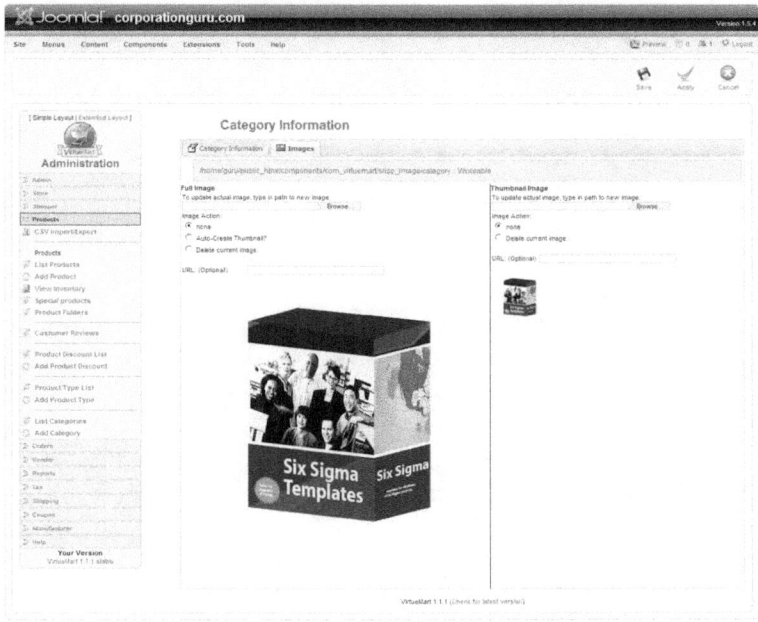

Now go change the rest of the categories to your topics.

Figure 189: Category Tree Guru

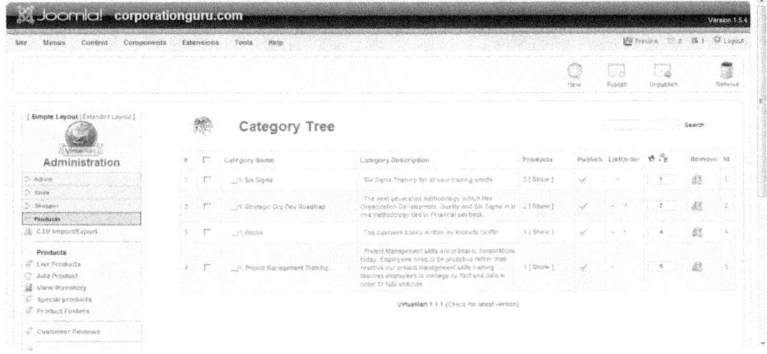

Virtuemart Manufacturer

We need to add a manufacturer. This is optional but looks nice on the website. Go to the Virtuemart Control Panel on the left hand navigation menu click on Manufacturer then list manufacturer.

Figure 190: Manufacturer list

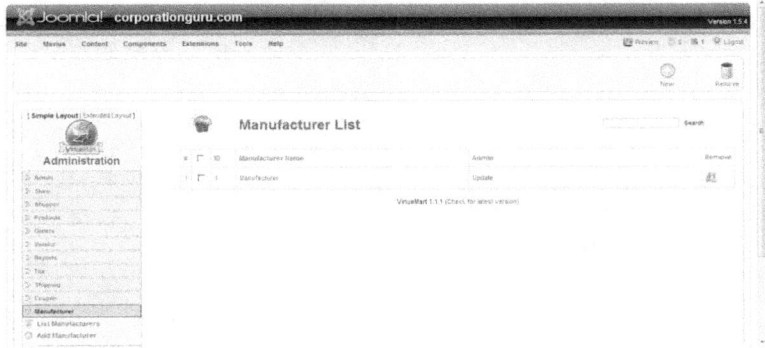

Click on Manufacturer Name to go to the details and add your manufacturers information.

Figure 191: Manufacturer Details

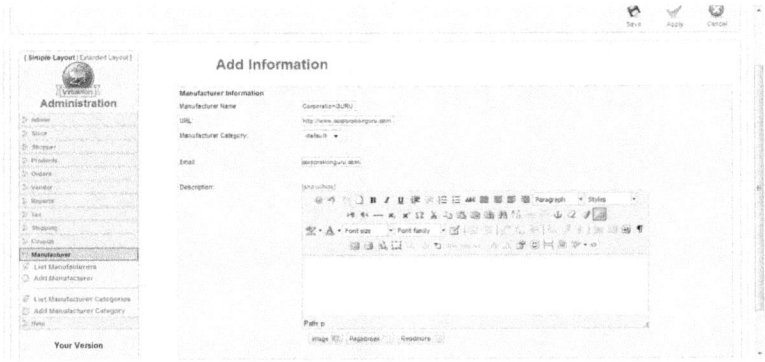

Virtuemart Products

There are three ways to add products (Product List, Product Folder and CSV). I will show you all three ways, in this chapter we will cover only the Product List and Product Folder. The first way is to go to the Product list. First go to the Virtuemart Control Panel and on the left hand navigation go to Products/List Products

Figure 192: Control Panel

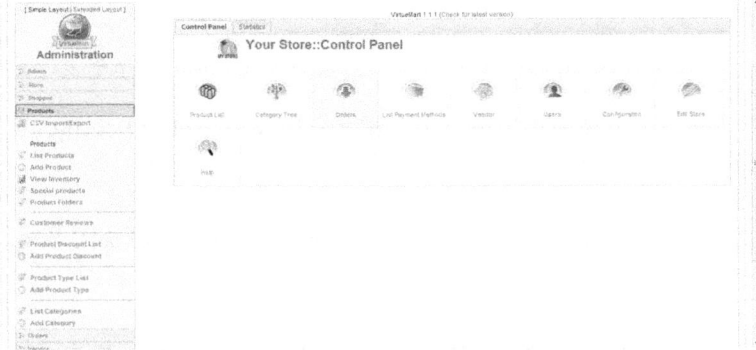

Figure 193: Product Listing

The second method is via Product Folders. If you look on the left hand navigation Product folders is located under Products.

Figure 194: Product Folders

When you click the item, it will go directly to the Product detail page, described in the next section.

Choose which method you like best and then we will begin to create a product.

Let's go into the detail of one of the default products and change it to one of our products. The Product Detail page is basic product information.

You will need to come up with a numbering scheme for your products in order to track inventory. These SKU numbers need to be unique.

There are two different philosophies in business. You will have to decide the proper method for your company. Once you decide on a direction it is hard to change within a fiscal year.

Therefore think through this process, especially if your website is for a growing business. Inventory numbering schemes:

• Smart Numbering, as your products structures grow with a large number of products you may want to use smart numbering. This could be alpha, numeric or a combination of both. For instance for my Six Sigma line, I have 6 products, therefore I could number the products: SSGB, SSBB, SSL, SSYB or SS01, SS02, SS03 where each number means a particular product.

• Consecutive Numbering, many large corporations use consecutive numbering because when you are dealing with 1000's of products, it becomes complicated to add new products to maintain consistent coding. Many organizations start with a 6 digit numbering scheme which goes up to 999,999 products. This leaves you plenty of room to grow and you may never max out on numbering.

Personally for CorporationGuru, we are going to use Smart Numbering, just to keep products segmented and also to think to the future, once segment of the corporation is sold off or separated in to a separate corporation, the product lines can be separated apart from the rest of the product lines.

Again, this is a personal decision, but once set it is very difficult to change as a company direction in the future.

For your product add your SKU number, Name, Category, Price, Discount (if applicable), Short Description and Long Description (at the bottom of the form).

I recommend you save after the first screen and then go back in to the next tab. I would hate for you to enter all the information then your session times out.

Figure 195: Product Details

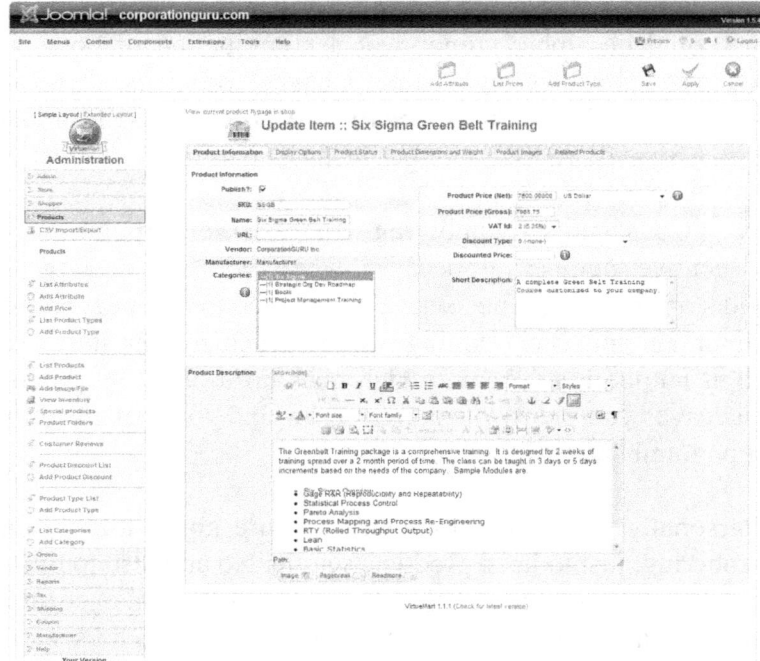

Figure 196: Display Values

The default is focused on the Parent items. You are able to uncheck this box and individually configure the items for child items. For initial design of your website, I recommend leaving this as default. As you build your products then you can tweak the settings.

The Quantity boxes are nice, because you can play with the way your customer selects product. You will need to play with the settings to see what works best. Since my products are bought individually then I will stay with the default. But if you sell products where customers could buy multiple units then a drop down box may be a better choice. Let's click on the next tab, product status.

Figure 197: Product Status

Figure 198: Website using Attributes

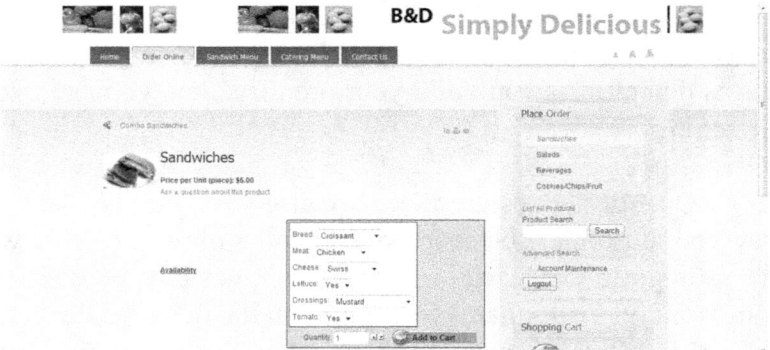

The Product Status page is packed full of features. Again, you will need to play with to see what works for you.

I basically get all the products in and then begin to tweak them, as I work the website, in order to make it customer focused.

Attached is an example of a website using the attribute (features and option selections) for a product.

Each attribute is a drop down box, this way the customer can select exactly what they want.

In the attribute space type in the name of the attribute and then add the property and if there is a price associated. If there are additional properties then click add.

Once you are done with the first attribute then click add attribute to add another.

Make sure you save frequently.

Figure 199: Product Attributes setup

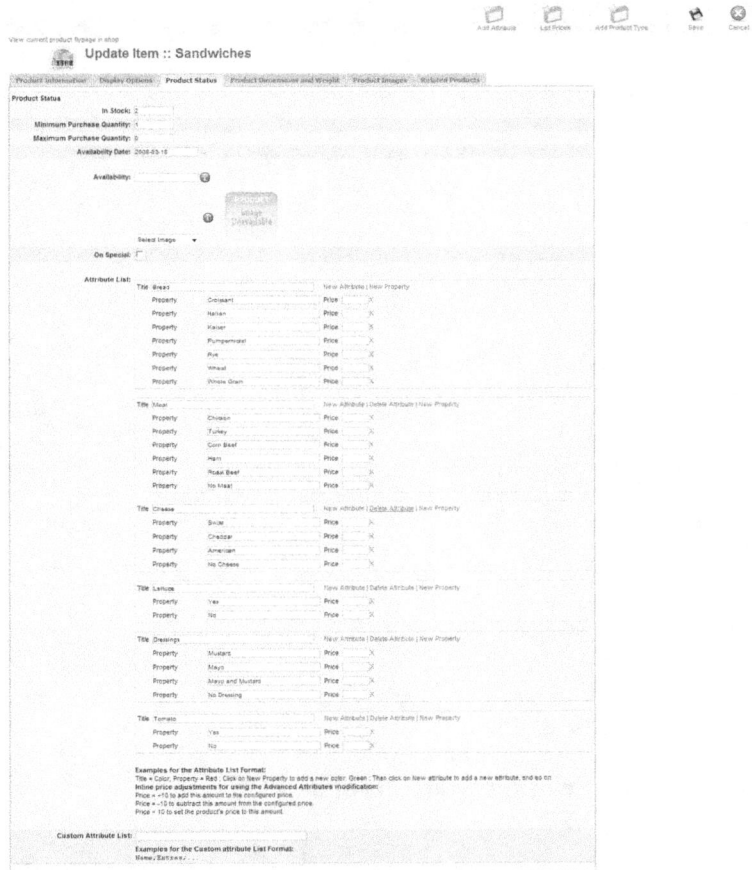

For CorporationGuru, I will not be using attributes. Therefore I deleted the attributes.

The sample invoice shows what an order looks like once a customer selects all their items. This is an actual business site at www.bdsimply.com who built it using Joomla 1.5.

Figure 200: Sample Invoice with Attributes

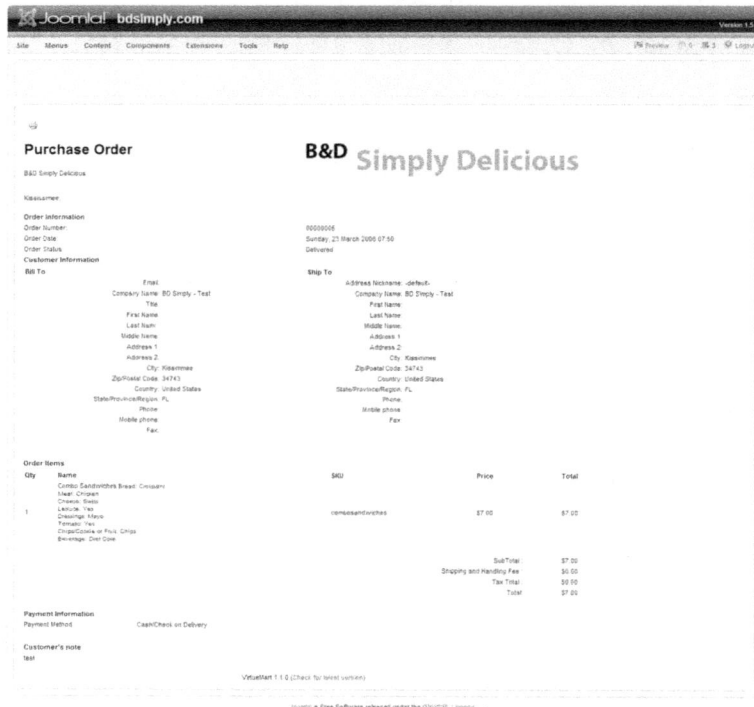

Figure 201: Product Status Guru

Next to Availability date there is ... - click on this for a calendar.

Make sure you have you product with a date in the past. Otherwise your product will not show up until the date it shows.

On Special is a neat little feature, this need to be checked if you want your product to show up under Featured.

Let's go to the next tab. Product Dimensions is an optional screen, but if you use the shipping modules it is good to have the dimensions entered.

Figure 202: Product Dimensions

The next tab is product image. This is similar to how we handled loading images in the Product Category chapter. Go ahead and load your image.

Figure 203: Product Image

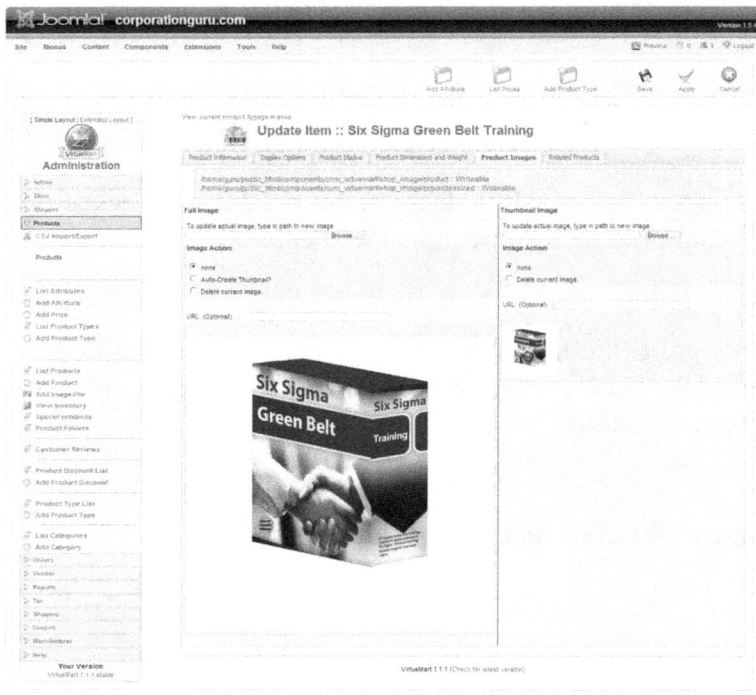

The last tab, Related Products you will need to fill out after you enter many of your products.

Figure 204: Related Products

To use this feature, just type in a key word for instance one of your categories and the selections come up. Then click on the products which are related (customers who bought this product also bought this product). Go ahead and update, a few more products in order to have an understanding how this area works.

Figure 205: Product Overview

Virtuemart Configuration Update

Refresh your website and notice how your Product Scroller and Product features now show your products and listings.

Now that we have activated the Virtuemart Login versus the Joomla login we need to make a few changes before we test the ordering process.

Now that Virtuemart is installed we need to change the Activate user account to NO. We do not want a customer placing an order then having to go back and approve their registration account. They could become frustrated and not place the order. Therefore we need to limit the frustration level.

We need to go to Cpanel and change the permissions on the configuration.php file to 777. Refer back to the Global Configuration chapter for changing the permissions.

Figure 206: Global Configuration update

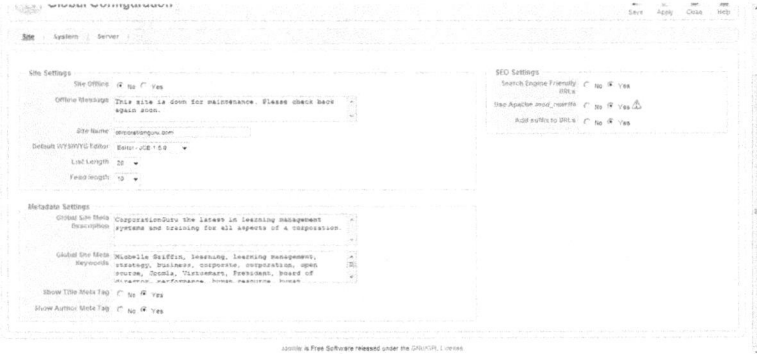

Once you change the permission, if you go to the Global Configuration file in Joomla – Site/Global Configuration you will notice User settings are now missing. This is because it is now handled through Virtuemart. Make sure once you change the files you need to go back into Cpanel and change the permissions back to 644. Due to Security concerns, never leave this file writeable

Figure 207: Virtuemart Configuration

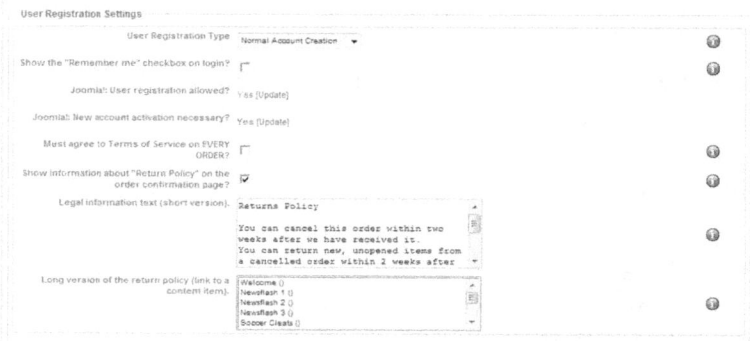

Since we can't make the change there now we have to go to the Virtuemart Control Panel. Then open the Configuration file under Admin. Scroll down to User Settings and click on the update link for Joomla! New account activation necessary.

Figure 208: Virtuemart Configuration updated

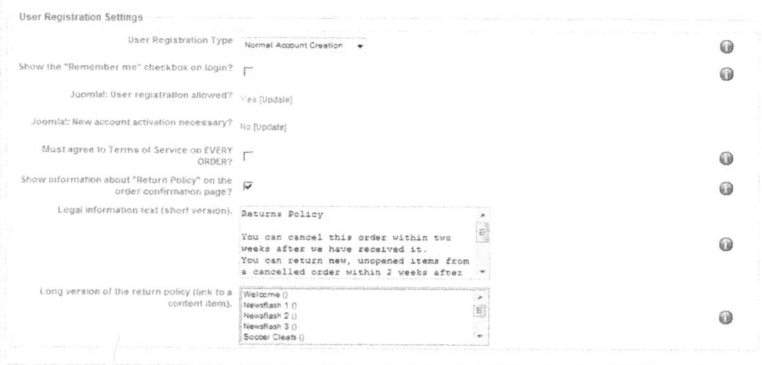

Figure 209: Joomla Global Configuration

Virtuemart Product Layout

Refresh your website. Let's click on the product category in order to look at the ordering process.

Figure 210: Website

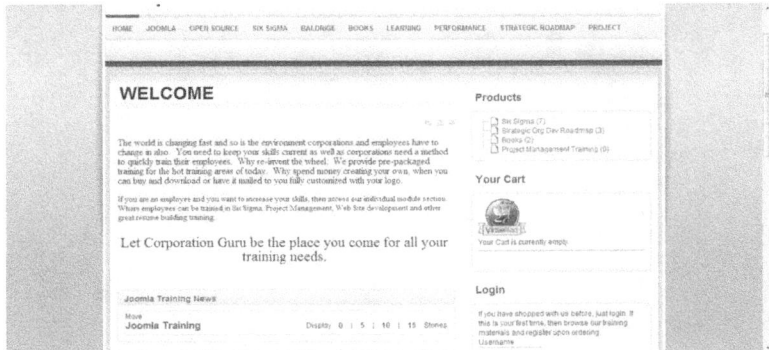

I clicked on the Six sigma link and when I looked at the page there were a few errors which need to be cleaned up. One the product listing of 3 across makes it look cluttered. Also, the Black Belt product is missing an order button lastly. So let's walk through and clean up this page.

Figure 211: Website 3 across

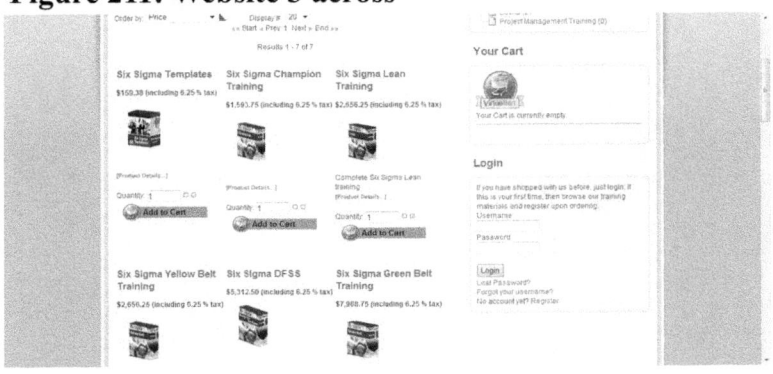

Figure 212: Product ordering page

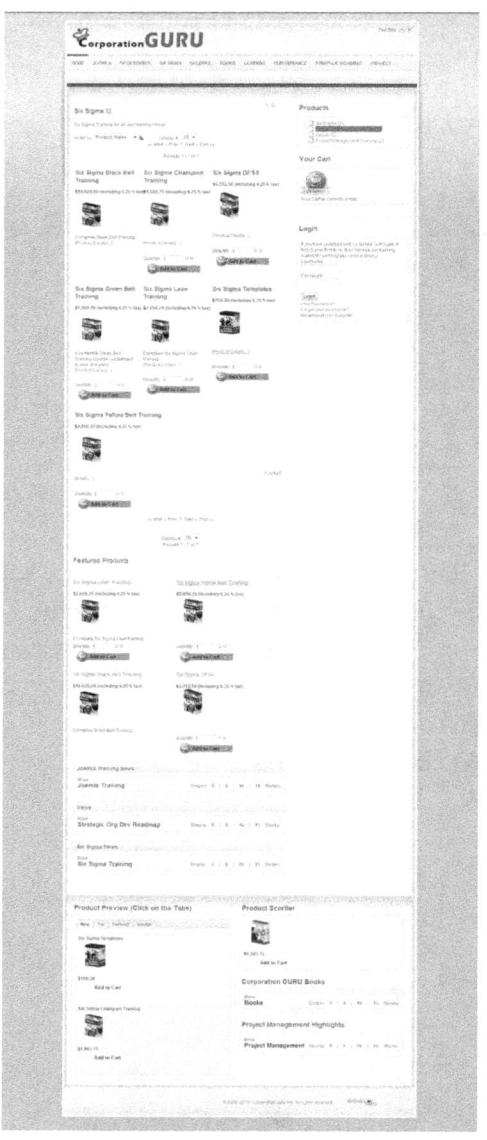

First, let's change the view to be 2 across. We need to go into
the Category Listing and change the display.

Figure 213: Category Tree

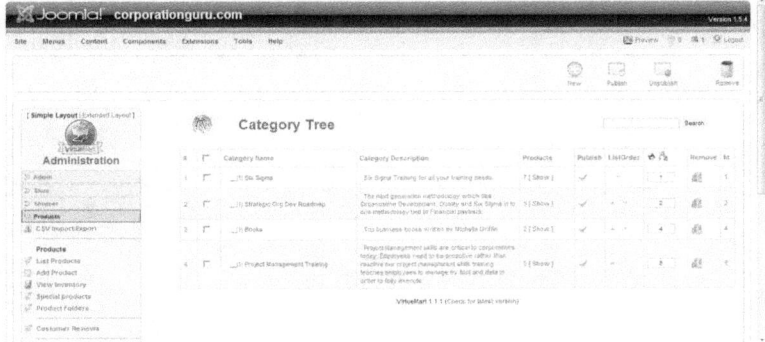

We are going to adjust the field "Show x products". I am going
to change it to 2 across and then save and refresh your website.

Figure 214: Category Detail

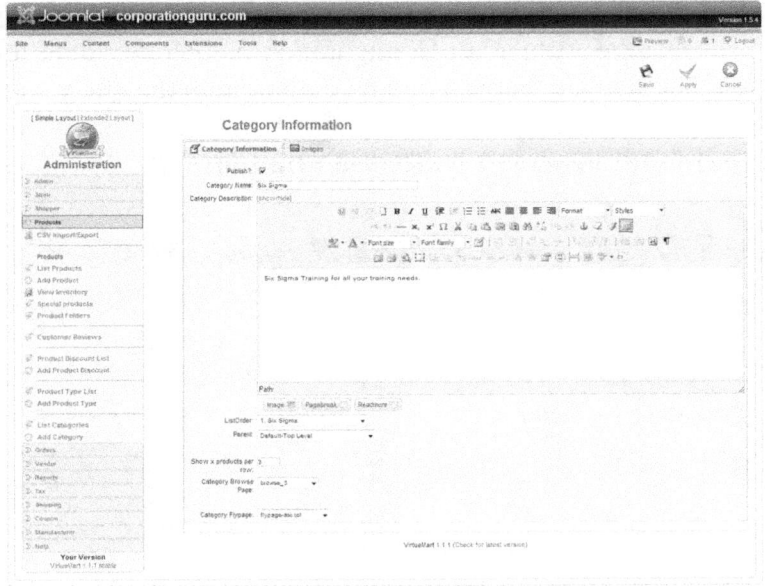

Figure 215: Website Products 2 across

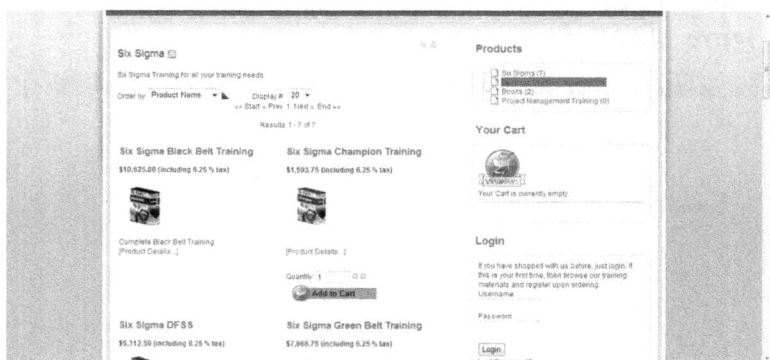

The next thing I will do is change the order of the product. There is a reorder buttons in the Product list, but these do not seem to work.

I suspect the Virtuemart Configuration file is overriding this. Given that they are there sometime in the future they may work.

Figure 216: Product List Reorder buttons

But to reorder product for now we need to go to Virtuemart Control Panel/ Admin/ Configuration

Figure 217: Configuration

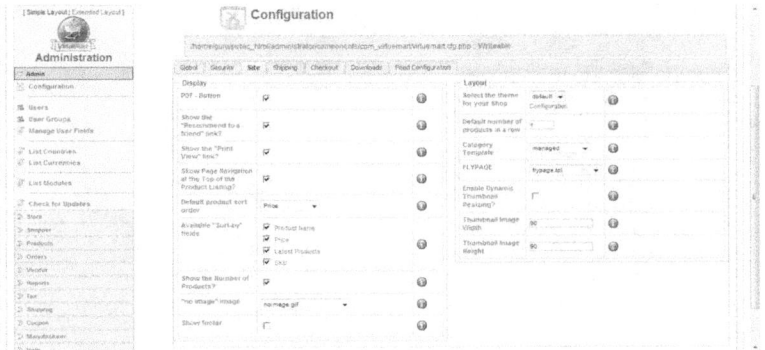

Within the Configuration file go to the Site tab, under "default product sort order" I had it set to product (which means alphabetically), I know changed it to price then save. This makes the order the way I wanted it.

I still have the problem with the Black belt product not showing a detail field.

The only thing I can think of is I changed the default item which had child items.

Therefore rather than continue to try and figure out what is the problem, because it could take hours; I am just going to create a new item and delete the old one.

It worked therefore we now are all set with the cosmetic changes.

Figure 218: Rearranged Layout

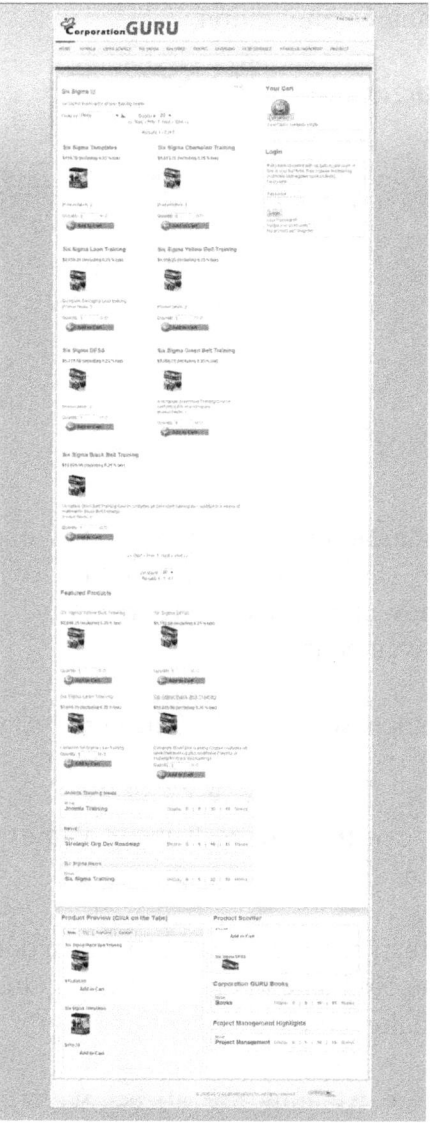

Virtuemart Browse Page Layouts

We are going to cover the browse page layouts located in the Category manager. There are just subtle differences.

But, you may find one you like better then the Browse_3 which is the default.

First let's go to the Category Tree this is located in the Virtuemart Control Panel under Products/List Categories then click on your main category and go to the detail page.

Figure 219: Category Detail

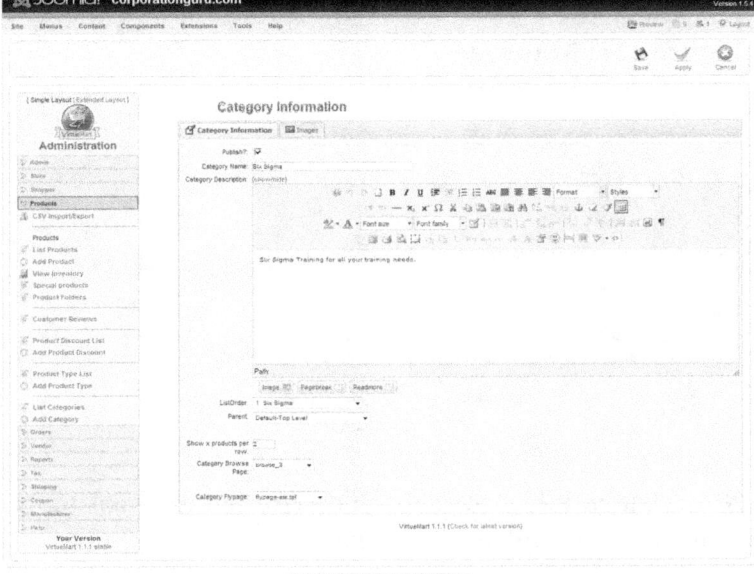

The Category Browse Page is set to Browse_3. We are going to change the browse pages and show you the differences.

Figure 220: Browse_3

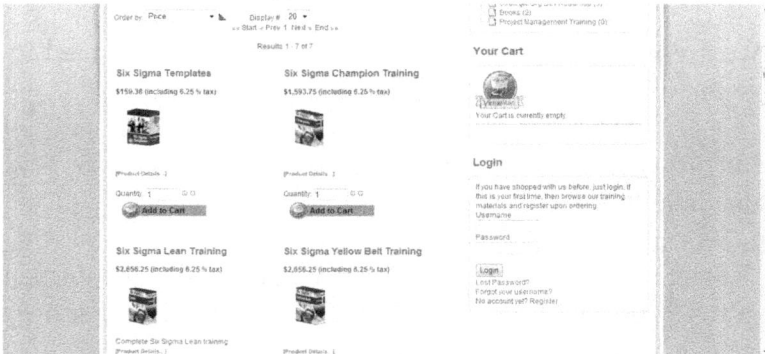

Let's changed it to Managed, and then refresh your website. Notice the Tax moves to below the image, the product details in next to the image and the Add to cart is moved to the right side.

Figure 221: Managed

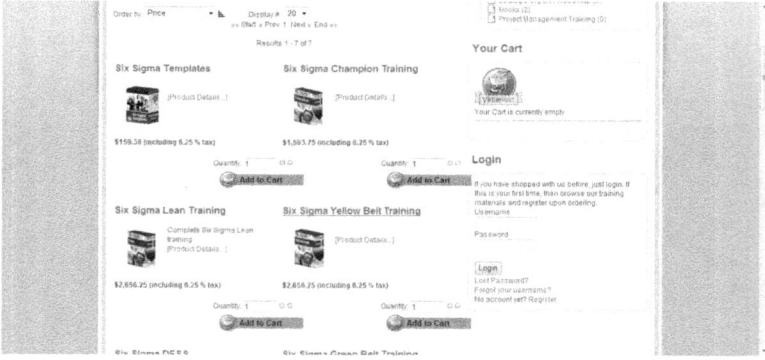

Now change it to Browse_1 and refresh your website. Notice the image moves up next to the name.

In order for this browse page to work you would need to disable the tax included in the configuration file.

Figure 222: Browse_1

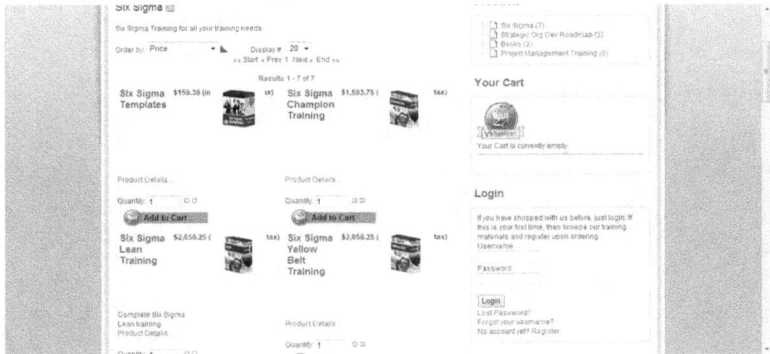

Let's try Browse_2 and refresh your website. The browse_2 looks like Managed, if there are differences it is very slight. Therefore let's look at what Browse_2 looks like as 1 across. Go back and change "Show x products across" to 1 then refresh your site. This makes the site pretty clean looking for customers. But, if you have a lot of products using this view, you would need to categorize your products a little more. For me I seem to like this view so far.

Figure 223: Browse_2

Let's try Browse_4 and change it back to 2 for products across.

Figure 224: Browse_4

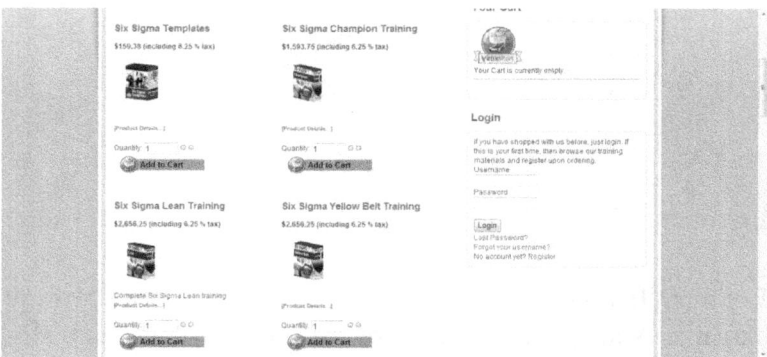

Change it now to Browse_5 and refresh the site. I like this but, it is missing the add to cart buttons. Therefore will not work for me.

Figure 225: Browse_5

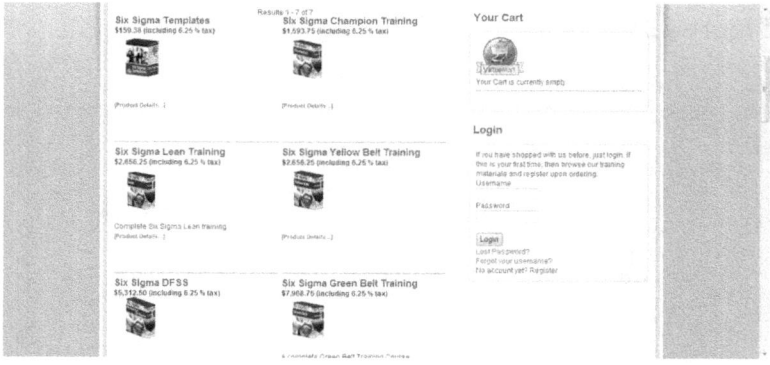

Lastly, let's change it to browse_lite_pdf. This one increased the font but is still missing the add to cart button.

Figure 226: Browse_lite_pdf

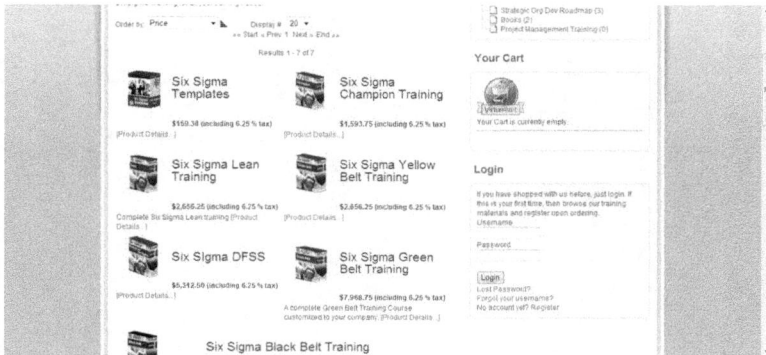

Go ahead and change your browse page to what fits your website.

Virtuemart Order Process

Let's place our first order and see how it looks. Go back to the home page of your website and let's start at the beginning of the ordering process.

Figure 227: Home Website

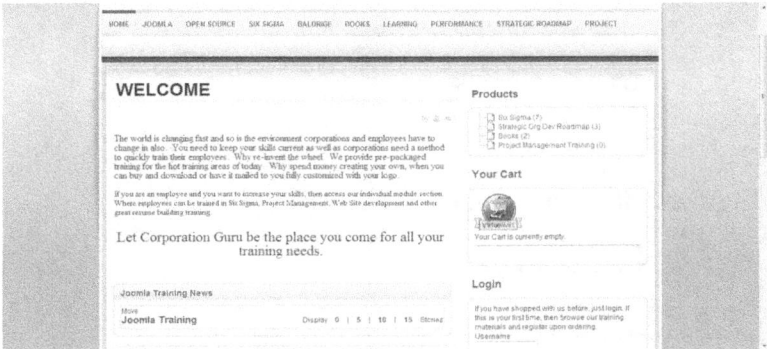

Then click on a products category.

Figure 228: Products Category

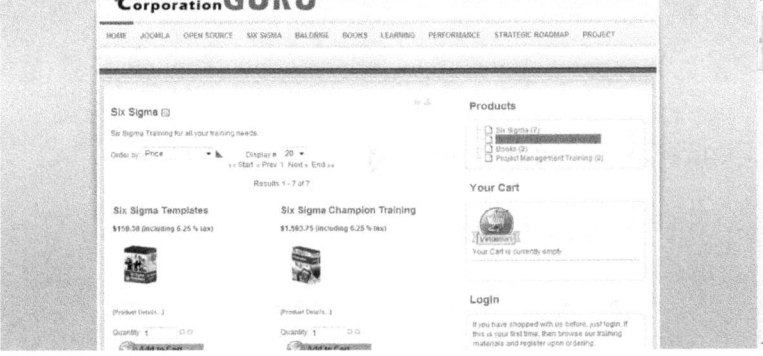

Add a few items to your cart. I am going to add 2 items to my cart. There are now 2 items in my cart. Notice the YOUR CART module now shows product. Next click on Show Cart

Figure 229: Cart Update

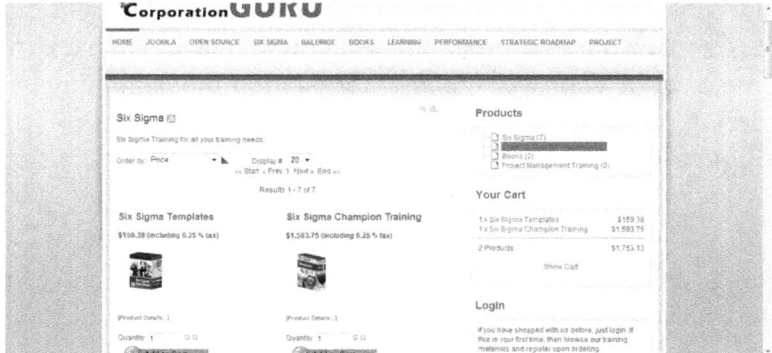

Figure 230: Show Cart

Figure 231: Update Quantity

Looks nice so far, now update quantity for one of your items and click the refresh button next to the quantity (arrows). I am going to change mine to 2.Let's delete one of the items to ensure the delete functionality works correctly.

Figure 232: Delete Item from Cart

Now, let's press checkout and begin the check out process. At this point, the customer needs to register or login.

Click on NEW, and the registration fields' popup. Field out the registration form with a user you had created an email or use a friends email. You need to verify the registration process works therefore you need access to the email. Then press Send registration.

Figure 233: Begin Registration

Figure 234: Registration process

We have proceeded to checkout step 1, once the registration was sent. Your customer will receive an email that they registered and you as the administrator will receive an email also.

Figure 235: User Registration to Customer

Figure 236: User Registration to Administrator

Figure 237: Checkout Step 1

Click Next to proceed to Step 2. I noticed on the Shipping I have not configured the shipping rates, I will need to go back and fix this. Otherwise I am going to proceed with this test order, go ahead and click next.

Figure 238: Step 2 Shipping

The order is ready to process, I noticed, that I need to rewrite the return policy, but otherwise everything looks good.

I recommend you write TEST in the "Please leave a Note box". Therefore you do not accidently try to process this order, go ahead and press confirm.

Figure 239: Step 3

Figure 240: Paypal

If you are using Paypal your Paypal screen should come up. For this order, I will just click on the link to return to the website.

The customer receives the following invoice for placing their order as well as the administrator is notified there is a new order. The email for notification is driven off the email in the Joomla Global configuration file.

Therefore this email needs to be an email which has the ability to service the customer when orders come in. If you set this email up as a generic email, for instance sales@corporationguru. com then many people could receive copies of the email, just by adding it to their Outlook account.

Figure 241: Customer Order Confirmation

If you click on the link at the bottom of the purchase order which came through the email, it takes the customer their order online in their account. They need to login when the link redirects them.

Figure 242: Online Order Confirmation

Congratulations, if you made it here with no errors you did everything correctly.

Virtuemart Order Status

Before we process this order, let's review order status types, this is a very nice feature in Virtuemart.

Order status types are important because it allows your customer and your back office people to be able to track the stages of orders. Order Status types are found in the Virtuemart Control Panel under Orders.

Figure 243: List Order Status Types

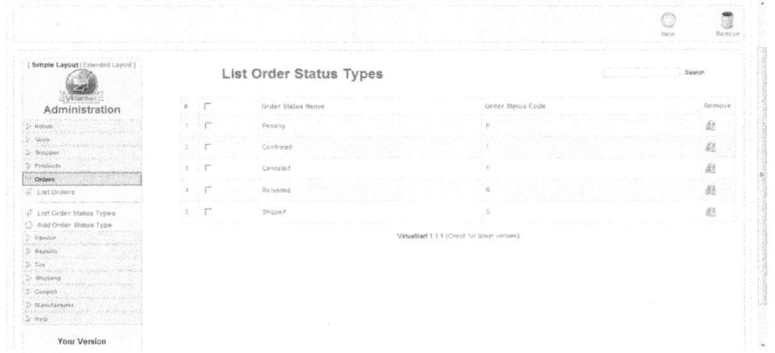

The Order Status types are customizable. But once orders are placed, it is not recommend you changed these. Therefore review these carefully to determine if they best suit your needs.

For instance, if you are running a Restaurant or a Customer pickups their product, instead of shipped you may want Delivered.

Based on the types of sites you are running, really dictates the types of steps which are required. For this example I am going to leave them as the default.

Figure 244: Order Status Detail

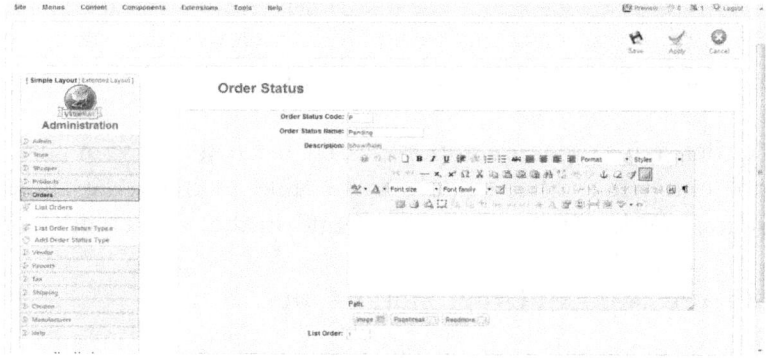

Virtuemart Orders

To access the Order processing screen, go to the Virtuemart Control Panel and click on List Orders under the Orders heading.

Figure 245: Order List

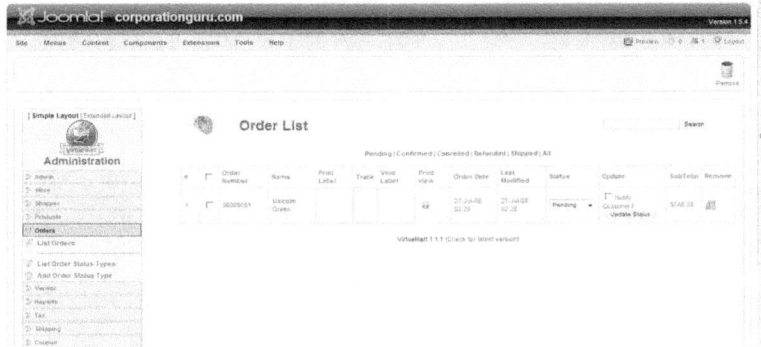

Click on the Order Number to access the order.

All the information you need on the order is on this screen. The payment information is at the bottom. Once you receive the order and begin processing it, you would want to confirm the order. Now, if you have different people the order process through, you may want to go back and add additional order status types at this time.

When you confirm the order the customer receives notification that the order has been accepted.

You can confirm the order from the Order listing or from the Order detail. If you do it at the order listing, then you need to check the box for Notify customer and click update status. This triggers the email to the customer. If you do it in the Order detail then you need to change the status and click update.

Figure 246: Order Detail

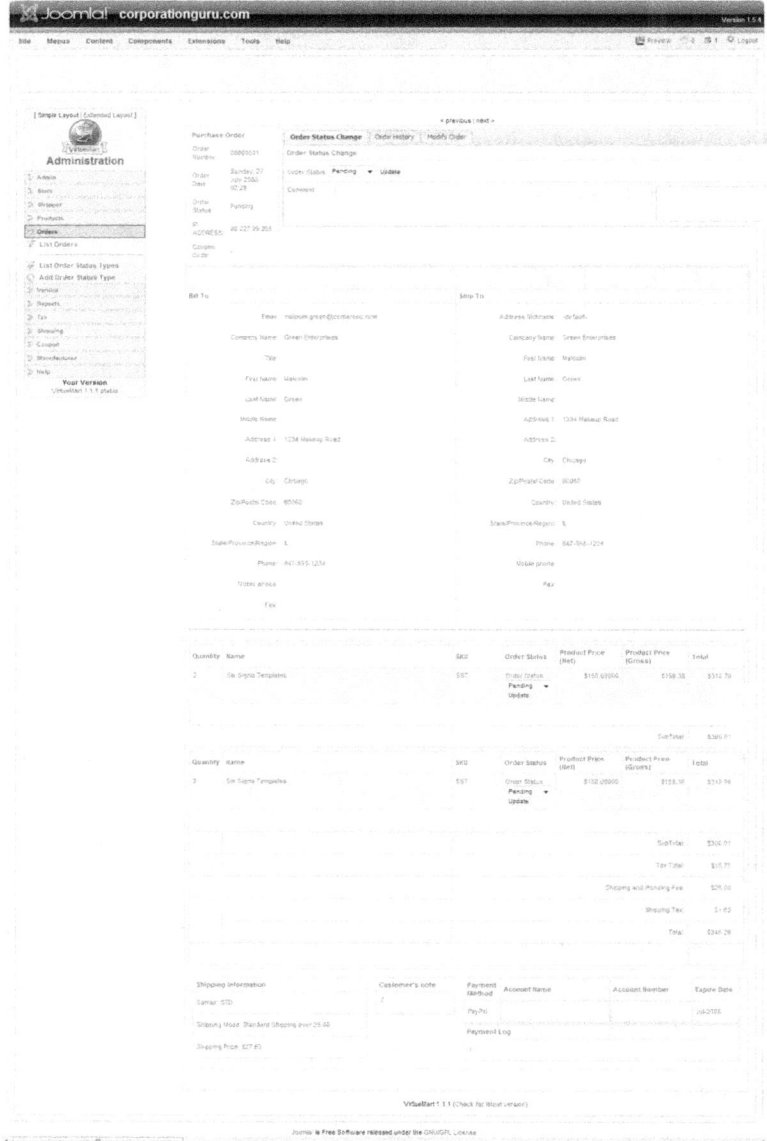

Figure 247: Order Status Confirmed Email

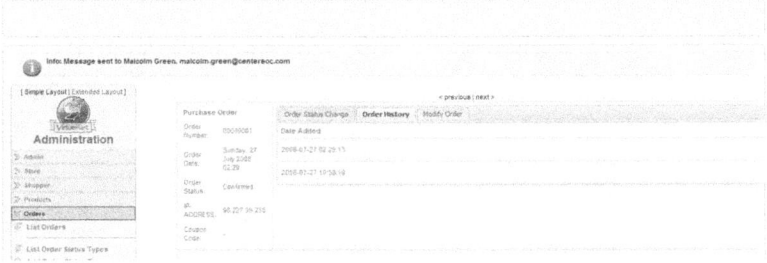

The Order History tab tracks the time any changes occur with the order. It does not tell you who made the change which would be a nice feature in the future. But it is nice to track what changes have occurred.

Figure 248: Order History

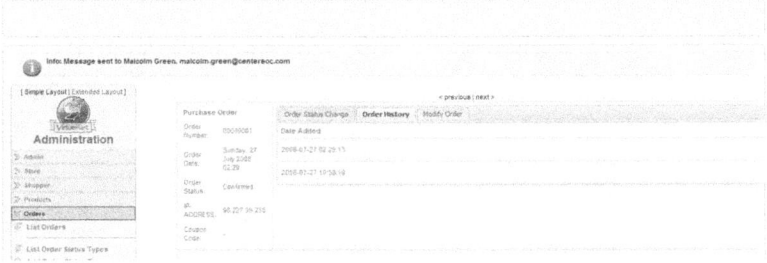

Once you ship the product then you will need to change this to shipped. There are nice little reports or you can extract your files at the end of the month, quarter or year in order to track your sales and to whom.

Virtuemart Inventory

Now that we have placed a sample order, we now need to go in and make sure the inventory is correct. Inventory was initially updated within the product detail. But it is easier to go to the inventory management screen. This is located in the Virtuemart Control Panel under Products/View Inventory

Figure 249: View Inventory

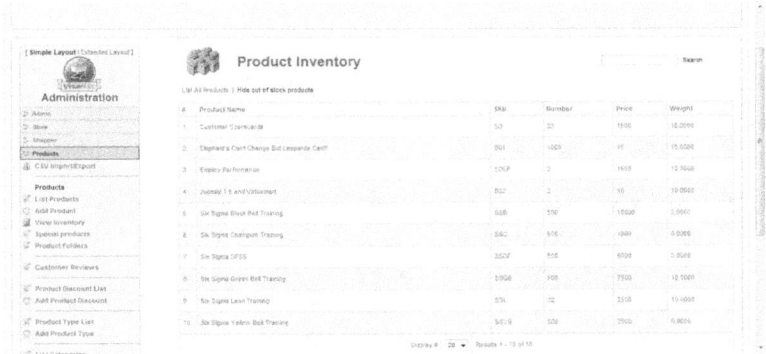

When you click on the product it brings you to the product detail screen, where you can adjust the inventory.

Figure 250: Product Detail Screen

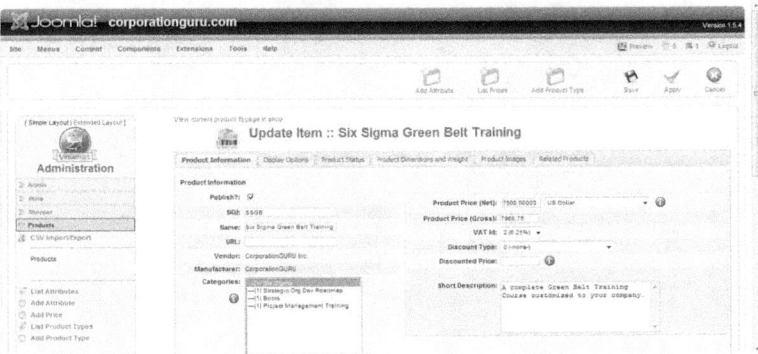

We do not have it setup to check inventory. If you run a business where you want the system to check available inventory prior to an order being placed, then you need to go back to the Admin/Configuration screen and under Inventory check the box for check inventory. This will not allow a user to add more inventory then what you have in stock to their cart.

Figure 251: Configuration

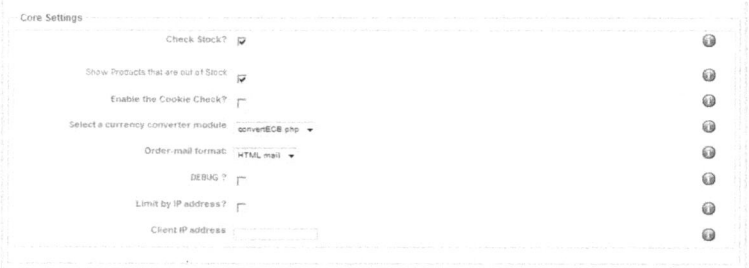

Virtuemart Report

There are online reports, which cannot be extracted at this time but they are handy to view what transactions have occurred for your business. The report is access in the Virtuemart Control Panel / Reports

Figure 252: Report Screen

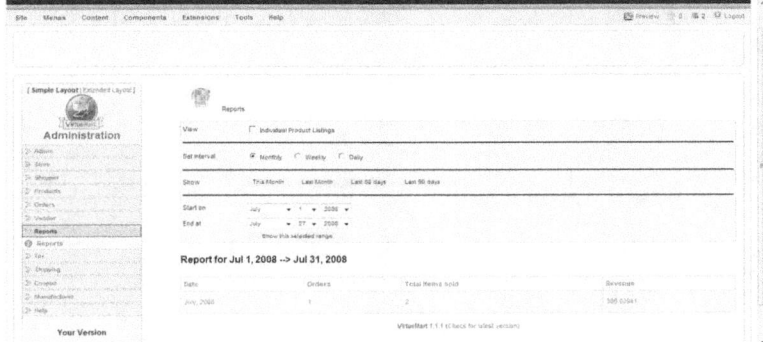

The reports can be ran daily, weekly or monthly. You can also check the box to view individual reports by product sold.

In order to run a report you need to select the time period, then either press one of the buttons in the Show row (this month, last month, last 60 days or last 90 days) or select a date range and press the button show this selected range.

Figure 253: Report by Product

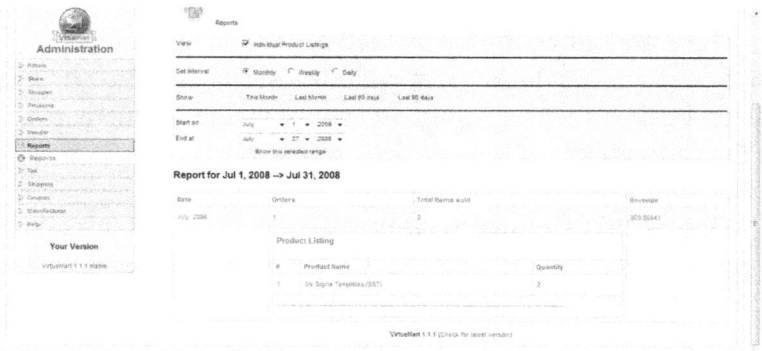

Virtuemart Account Maintenance

Once your customer logs in they are able to track their orders and modify their profile. The account maintenance link is located in the login box once the customer login. Let's login to the account we used for the test order.

Figure 254: Website login

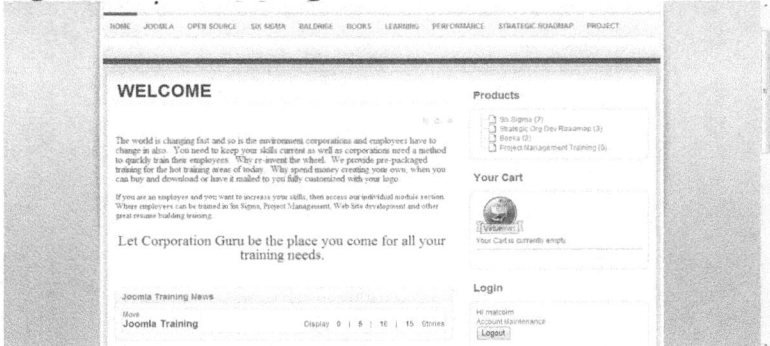

Once login then click on Account Maintenance. Your customer can view their account information and order history as well as their status.

Figure 255: Account Maintenance

Click on Account Information to view the detail.

Figure 256: Account Information

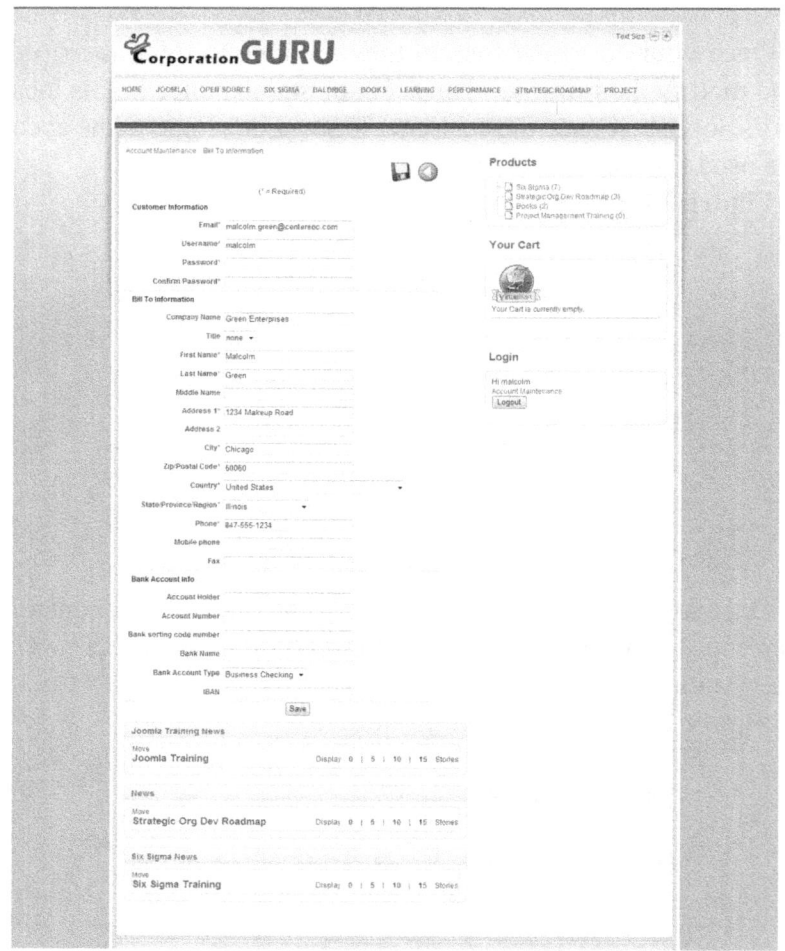

Even though you are at the end of the this book you have developed skills, which now allow you to go further with your website. If you have any questions, I am always willing to answer them contact me at 1-847-848-5857 or email michelle.griffin@ corporationguru.com.

Biography

Currently, Michelle Griffin 44, is Chief Operating Officer of the C.E.O.C. Corporation. The mission is "creating innovation solutions to everyday global business issues."

Prior to this appointment, Griffin had served since August 2003 as Vice President of Customer Experience where she spent four years improving the service revenue and profitability, managing a $750 million dollar, service revenue stream for Océ North America, Inc. Her focus was on revenue, customer retention, and visual performance management dashboards.

Prior to this, she was Senior Vice President Group Operations at Bank of America. She served five years as Chief Information Officer for Instanet Manufacturing Corporation. Michelle consulted for over 15 years as a firefighter on Baan and SAP Implementations. Working as a Sub-contractor for Deloitte and Touche, Cooper and Lybrand and Arthur Anderson.

Michelle was called in when a Baan or SAP implementation was struggling due to special requirements of the software or the processes.

She received her Undergraduate degrees from Broome Community College and Binghamton Univerisity. Binghamton University is where she received her MBA in 1986. Michelle is currently finishing her Doctorate at Benedictine University, in Chicago. Her Doctorate is in Organization Development.

Michelle's expertise is in profitability of corporations and has a deep understanding of organizations, financially and operationally.

She is industry independent, because business is business. She has consulted and worked in many industries from Banking, Automative, Service to a variety of "Make to Order environments."

Michelle loves speaking at conferences and corporation meetings. If you wish to invite Michelle to your next conference please contact her at 1-800-883-5102 or 1-847-848-5875.

Index

Coupons

With the purchase of Joomla 1.5 & Virtuemart book, you are entitled to 1 free logo for your website. All you have to do is provide proof of purchase. A graphic design project manager will call you from Corporation GRAPHIC and will work with you in designing your logo.

This is a $150 dollar value!

You will have all rights to your logo and it can be used for your website as well as printed materials.

With the purchase of Joomla 1.5 & Virtuemart book, you are entitled to 3 months free wehhosting for 1 website. Upon verification of proof of purchase your website will be available within 1 hour of contacting Spiderweby personnel. You will have to set your nameservers, through your domain registrar.

ns1.spiderweby.net
ns2.spiderweby.net

The Spiderweby staff will also provide phone support during your initial setup of your website, as you learn to build your website using the Joomla! 1.5 & Virtuemart book.

This is a $150 dollar value!

You will have all rights to your logo and it can be used for your website as well as printed materials.

Free Webhosting is for non-commercial or commercial sites. Adult sites are prohibited, as well as sites focused on spamming.

At the end of 3 months, you may sign up for a month to month hosting at $6.95 a month or $70 dollars a year.

Webhosting Features	
Setup	CPanel
Add On Domains	Parked Domains
Sub Domains	FTP Accounts
Online User Accounts	Customized Error Pages
Customer Account Page	24/7/365 Support
FTP Session Control	Latest Visitor Log
Webalizer	Redirects

Email Features	
Unlimited Emails	Pop3- Your Website
SMTP - Your website	IMAP
Easy Email Account Setup	Default Address
User Level Filtering	Account Level Filtering
Email Delivery Route	Forwarders
MX Entry	Responders
Web Mail	Mailing List
Mass Mail	Spam Assassin
Catch-all Address	

Technological Features	
Storage	Bandwidth
MySQL	Front Page Extensions
Dreamweaver Compatible	CGI Bins
99.9% Uptime	Offsite Disaster Recovery
Tape Backup	Power Generator
Redundancy	Backups
Backup Wizard	File Manager
Disk Space Usage Monitor	Web Disk

Extra Features	
Fantastico	PHP My Admin
Perl Support	PHP Pear
SSI - Server Side Includes	Ruby on Rails Support
Macromedia Support	Adobe Support
Midi Support	Real Media Support
Audio Support	Streaming Video
Flash Support	IP Deny Manager
Imaage Manager	Index Manager